ODI ET AMO

The Complete Poetry of Catullus

The Library of Liberal Arts
OSKAR PIEST, FOUNDER

ODI ET AMO

The Complete Poetry of

CATULLUS

Translated, with an introduction, by

ROY ARTHUR SWANSON

. . . .

The Library of Liberal Arts

published by

Macmillan Publishing Company
New York
Collier Macmillan Publishers
London

Caius Valerius Catullus: *c.* 84-54 B.C.

Macmillan Publishing Company
866 Third Avenue
New York, New York, 10022

First Edition
Eighteenth Printing — 1987

Library of Congress Catalog Card Number: 59-11685
ISBN: 0-02-418490-X

CONTENTS

· · · · · · · · · · · · · · · · ·

FOREWORD

Caius (pronounced "Gay-us") Valerius Catullus, who lived, it seems, from about 84 to 54 B.C., is the first great name in the history of Roman lyricism, the greatest name in this history, in fact, if we define lyric poetry as stanzaic or schematic verse expressive of the poet's feeling or of emotions in general. Of the Roman poets who follow Catullus in lyricism—Horace, Tibullus, Propertius, and Ovid—none is quite so expressive of personal feeling as he. All except the temperate Horace follow Catullus in his disregard of conservative Roman ideals (for example, the serious and practical life) and in his preoccupation with the pleasures and pains of love. But none remains so thoroughly subjective as Catullus, for whom the emotion of love was life itself.

Catullus was a romantic poet. That is to say, his state of mind produced an intensification and an idealization of human affairs, and he defined this state of mind in impeccable verse.

Caius Valerius Catullus, like Percy Bysshe Shelley, lived for three decades. For Catullus, as for a number of romantic poets, it was possible at the age of thirty to say *vixi*, I have lived (and am therefore dead). The romantic's third decade is often followed by death (e.g., Keats at 26, or even Byron at 36) or loss of the romantic impulse (e.g., Wordsworth), which is a form of death, or incipient melancholia marked by autobiographical introspection (e.g., Villon, Dylan Thomas). Living half of one's years may be a natural result of living with doubled intensity. And doubled intensity in the environment of youth is characteristic of the unashamed romantic, not only the poet but also the novelist (e.g., F. Scott Fitzgerald, Thomas Wolfe) or the soldier (e.g., Alexander the Great, Custer). At thirty, Catullus could say *vixi* and also *amavi* (I have loved and therefore do so no more). The death of Catullus' intense and idealized love for "Lesbia" was just short of coinciding with his physical death. If we think in this manner, we are less likely to be concerned with the inconsistent reports on the Roman poet's life span. For those of us who are being introduced to Catullus in English translation it is more important to know that he died young in the Rome of Cicero, Pompey, and Caesar after a life of heightened creative and amatory activity than that his dates are very likely 84-54 B.C., but may possibly be 87-54 B.C., or even 88 or 85 to 55 B.C.

Such biographical details as are essential to a consideration of Catullus can be limited to the personalities with whom he came into contact. These are the objects toward which he directs his intensity; and his lyrics provide a record of this direction. The most important personalities include "Lesbia," the neoteric poets, Caius Licinius Calvus, the brother of Catullus, Juventius, Marcus Caelius Rufus, Cicero, and Caesar.

"Lesbia" was the woman who meant more to Catullus than life. Her name is a poetic invention. Catullus, who adapted one of Sappho's poems to express his early admiration for this woman (see poem 51), came to associate her in name with the great Greek poetess of Lesbos. "Lesbia" was married but had obviously little time for her husband. It was probably through her husband that she first met Catullus. Very possibly she accompanied her husband on an official visit from Rome to Catullus' father in Verona. In the presence of these three, Catullus may have conceived his idea for poem 51. "Lesbia" apparently encouraged his versifying and his attentions. It is even possible that she had already known of his poetic reputation. Catullus was certainly a learned young man, well grounded in the Greek language and in late Greek, or Alexandrian, poetry. Poems 64 and 66, in particular, are patterned after the Alexandrian mode of poetic composition. Whatever the situation, she enjoyed a love affair with the poet when he met her in Rome. To Catullus she was unique and all that he desired in the province of love. But gradually her nymphomaniacal relations with his "rivals" left the disillusioned young man in a wake of torment. Reconciliations proved short-lived, and it appears that Catullus rejected a last offer of one on "Lesbia's" part with his second poem in the Sapphic meter (poem 11). There is reason to believe that "Lesbia" was the notoriously free-living Clodia, wife of Quintus Metellus Celer, a conservative Roman consul in 60 B.C. who died under suspicious circumstances in the year following his consulship, and sister of Publius Clodius Pulcher, a highborn political racketeer in the hire of Julius Caesar.

It was against the likes of Clodius and Caesar that the neoteric or "newcomer" poets directed lampoons and general versified abuse. This group of erudite young men from northern Italy specialized, however, in the production of a highly schematized narrative verse which has come to be called epyllionic. Their models were the Alexandrian writers. Catullus, Calvus, and Caelius Rufus were a part of this avant-garde.

Catullus' poem 64 is a good example of the "epyllion." The schematization involves a balance of themes or topics. The first thirty lines introduce the figures of Peleus and Thetis, who are to be married with the full consent of the gods. The age in which Peleus and Thetis lived was a mythological age of heroes, and the moral fiber of men was then strong. This was the age of the Golden Fleece expedition. The poem closes as it opens, with a consideration of past glories. The last twenty-five lines berate human corruption subsequent to the time when gods held concourse with men. The wedding day in all its splendor takes up the lines 31-49. The human guests are accounted for and attention is called to the palace adornments and the wedding couch. This section is balanced by lines 267-382, which present the departure of the human guests, the arrival of the divine guests, and the song of the Fates (Parcae). Lines 50-51 mention figures embroidered on the coverlet of the wedding couch. One of these figures is Ariadne. Thereupon Catullus tells the story of Ariadne and Theseus (lines 52-264). This is the central portion of the entire poem; it is, of course, a digression. But the digression is an epyllionic requirement and it is thematically unobtrusive: the unhappy love of Ariadne and Theseus is contrasted with the bliss of Peleus and Thetis; furthermore, Bacchus' rescue of Ariadne on Naxos testifies to divine interest in human affairs. At the close of the story a second pair of lines are devoted to the coverlet embroidery. We have observed, then, the following scheme:

Heroic and high moral character of the contemporaries of Peleus and Thetis.

Wedding day of Peleus and Thetis. Human guests.

Coverlet embroidery.

Story of Ariadne and Theseus.

Coverlet embroidery.

Wedding day of Peleus and Thetis. Divine guests.

Unheroic and immoral character of the poet's contemporaries.

Poem 68 can be similarly analyzed.

The pleasure and interest of the neoterics in appreciating the recognizable talent of each other is echoed in Catullus' poem 50. This poem concerns Catullus' delight in the company of C. Licinius Calvus, a neoteric who is known to have composed an epyllionic poem based on the Io story. Calvus was also a very successful orator (i.e., lawyer). His brilliant oration against a corrupt official, Vatinius, (see poem 53) may have taken place about 54 B.C. If so, it would mean that Catullus could not have died before this year; but, of more importance, it would indicate that this strong friendship was ended only by the death of Catullus. Poem 50 shows overtly how ingenuous and sincere Catullus could be in his personal relations. Both his loves and his dislikes and hates are expressed with an equally extreme lack of reserve. Translators and commentators too frequently interpret this lack of reserve as childlike naïveté. Catullus is not naïve; he is romantic and honest. He is not a child, but a sensitive adult.

The intensity of Catullus' emotion in love, in hate, and in friendship is again seen in his fraternal devotion. Catullus' brother died and was buried in the Troad. He managed to visit his brother's grave during, or as the result of, a short term of military government duty in Asia Minor in the year 57 B.C. The extent of his grief is discernible in poems 101 and 68. His fraternal love, frustrated by his brother's death, is balanced in its extremity by an extreme hatred directed against an almost personified Troad.

Intensity again characterizes Catullus' homosexual love for the boy Juventius. And again his frustration results in the extremity of hate. It is easy enough to note the pattern of the poet's love and hate: he loves A but, in losing A, always aims his hatred at B before fully identifying it with A. He loves "Lesbia," but hates his rivals for her affections before he hates "Lesbia" herself. He loves Juventius, but hates his rivals for the boy's affection before turning on Juventius himself (see poem 106, presumably a Juventian poem).

One of his rivals for the love of "Lesbia" was his erstwhile friend, Marcus Caelius Rufus (see poems 58, 73, 77). The published complicity of Caelius and Clodia seems to validate the identification of "Lesbia" with Clodia. The story of Caelius and Clodia is devastatingly clarified in Cicero's famous defense of Caelius (*Pro Caelio*). Clodia had charged Caelius with conspiracy in an attempted poisoning. Cicero called the notice of the court to Clodia's favors and attentions toward Caelius, who actually lived in her Palatine home, ably reminded the court of Caelius' integrity, and hinted quite effectively that Clodia herself may certainly have used poison to accelerate the demise of her husband, the august Metellus. Caelius was acquitted.

Cicero himself was singled out for praise by the neoterics, whose political sympathies gave way to ostensible admiration for the man openly and vigorously opposed to Caesar. Catullus, for example, praises the oratorical abilities of Cicero in poem 49.

The years 59-49 B.C. were Caesar's years so far as the fortunes

of Rome were concerned. Catullus died in the middle of
Caesar's decade. His attitude toward the conqueror of Gaul
is initially one of conventional neoteric spite and contempt.
But he seems to have given this up in favor of tolerance and
respect. Caesar is said to have entertained Catullus at one
time. Whether it was this or merely political pressure that
effected the change in Catullus' attitude cannot be deter-
mined at present. It is, at any rate, unwise to suggest that
Catullus ever hated Caesar with the same intensity that he
hated his rivals in the affairs of "Lesbia" and Juventius or
even the poetasters of his day (e.g., Aquinus, Hortensius,
Suffenus, Volusius). His animosity may have been no more
severe than that of present-day political cartoonists toward
the objects of their lampoons.

Catullus appears most to *hate* Caesar when he uses his in-
fallible instrument of hatred, obscenity, to deride him. Catul-
lus is often jocularly obscene. But he is more frequently
vindictively obscene; it is this brand which carries over into
his anti-Caesarian lines. In its fullest strength his obscenity
abuses his rivals and those who have insulted or humiliated
him. In its fullest strength we see Catullan intensity at its
peak and in fitting complement to the poetic instruments of
his love and friendship.

A substantial fraction of the Catullan poems are "obscene"
or viciously vituperative. Commentators tolerate these, explain
them away (as, for instance, emphasizing that the verbs are
here not to be understood in the literal sense, but only as
conveying vague threats, in the gross language of that day),
or overlook them. None will *praise* them. And yet these are as
decidedly Catullan as the overpraised but praiseworthy
"sparrow" poems (2, 3). I should like to submit that some
praise is owing even to such a blatantly vile poem as 97. After
all, imagery is seldom quite so forceful, comparisons are
seldom so vividly presented.

Praise might also be reserved for other Catullan poems that
are commonly slighted. The last four lines of poem 51, for ex-
ample, receive little critical acclaim in the rush to brand them

as intruders (since they apparently have negligible connection with the preceding three stanzas). The Latin has the word *otium* (sloth, idleness) introduce the first three lines:

Otium . . .

otio . . .

otium . . . .

With this conventional anaphoric emphasis Catullus expresses his inability to get away from sloth. It weighs down every line. In degree, it ruins (1) him, (2) all his actions, and (3) kings and great cities. Sloth builds upon itself in terrifying aspect. Each line ends with the conventional and effective sibilant of contempt:

. . . *est*

. . . *gestis*

. . . *beatas*

. . . *urbes.*

The reader who is unfamiliar with Catullus will, I think, derive the greatest benefit from reading poem 64 before any other, by reading the poem thoroughly and repeatedly. It is the longest and greatest of Catullus' poems. I say this as confidently as Horace Gregory says, "Of the longer poems the marriage hymns are notably the best." The finest qualities of Catullan poetry are all to be found in this "epyllion." There is the architectural symmetry already noted, skillful use of refrain and apostrophe, sustained lyric, harsh invective, color, learning, and brilliant metrics (in the Latin, that is). And, being removed from the immediate area of Catullus' temperamental fall-out, it is externalized; universalized, if you will. Having reacted to the artistry of 64, we shall, in passing on to the short poems, look for (and invariably find) artistry rather than only the man.

The marriage hymns should be read next: poems 61, 62. One can envision the actual singing of them at colorful wedding celebrations. Here is more poetry of the highest rank.

Catullus should be read, in other words, from the top down, from impersonal artistry to personal artistry.

Catullus probably gained his reputation by producing poems of the caliber of 64 and the wedding songs. But he remains best known today for his superlatively intense session with love. He read a profound significance into his devotion for "Lesbia." This love was for him not just sex; it was akin to the instincts of immortality felt by men with respect to their progeny. The sexpot "Lesbia" had no desire to commune with immortality and Catullus found himself competing with lowbrow rivals: Quintius, Ravidus, Egnatius, Gellius, not to mention "Lesbius," the girl's own brother. The story of this love can be traced by reading the "Lesbia cycle": poems 51, 2, 3, 5, 7, 86, 83, 92, 70, 87, 104, 85, 72, 107, 36, 109, 82, 40, 39, 37, 58, 77, 78a, 73, 75, 8, 79, 60, 76, 11. (The ordering of these poems is my own and definitely does not echo scholarly concord hereto. The interested reader will, I know, rearrange them to suit himself.)

The "Gellius cycle" is a good follow-up to the "Lesbia cycle." The insults slung at his rival are a satisfactory introduction to Catullus' invective: poems 116, 74, 80, 88, 89, 90, 91.

The "Juventius cycle" (poems 99, 48, 15, 21, 16, 26, 23, 24, 81) illustrates another aspect of Catullan devotion, already mentioned above—namely, his homosexual attention to a handsome young family associate. In this affair his rivals are Aurelius and Furius, the two messengers who fail to effect a reconciliation between him and "Lesbia," once Catullus had realized for good and all that he had had it (see poem 11).

The other fires beneath the emotion of Catullus already alluded to are his bereavement of a brother (poems 101, 65, and parts of 68) and his attitude toward Julius Caesar (poems 29, 54, 57, 93, 11).

His sensitive delight in the company of C. Licinius Calvus (poems 14, 50, 53, 96) seems to be almost the only pleasure left untainted by disillusion.

The reading sequence outlined above will provide the un-initiated reader some systematic acquaintance with Catullus, and it will help to prevent the tedious confusion of mere browsing. I have respected the patently unchronological manuscript arrangement of the poems simply because this disposition is part and parcel of the Catullus that has been preserved to us.

Montaigne's observation that every man is a complete set of contradictions is eminently applicable to Catullus. One has only to juxtapose a "sparrow" poem and a Gellius poem to understand this. The collected poems of Catullus depict a life of doubled intensity, one in which learning, friendship, love, and hate are magnified or telescoped in the extreme while being subjected to precise and honest metrical and lyrical definition. Catullus knows the glories of divine concourse and the ugliness of gross sexuality. He gives expression to both in a variety of poetic forms. What may appear to some readers to be an irresolute contradiction in temperament is, in fact, temperamental integrity. Catullus is honest and is too much the complete poet to give us only his best side.

The entire Catullan collection was saved from extinction by one lone manuscript unearthed in Verona around the year 1311. Without it, the work of Catullus would be represented today only by poem 62, preserved in a ninth century manuscript. The Verona manuscript (called V) was lost, but not before copies of it had been made. Two of these, whether they are direct copies or at a near remove from the original, exist today. One is being kept in the National Library in Paris, the other in Oxford University's Bodleian Library. They are called, respectively, G (*Codex Sangermanensis,* dated about 1375) and O (*Codex Oxoniensis,* undated but almost certainly of the fourteenth century). In 1896, W. G. Hale discovered in the Vatican library another manuscript, now called R, which he claimed was copied along with G from a lost copy of the lost V. There are a few other extant manuscripts of a later date (fifteenth century) than T (the ninth century manuscript), O, and G, and therefore of less value. Scholars still debate the relative value of O and G, as well as the date of R. I bring these details in, however, simply to note the ultimate sources of this translation, in preparing which I have regularly consulted, in addition to a photolithographed reproduction of G (Paris, 1890), the critical editions of C. Lachmann (third edition, 1874), R. Ellis (second edition, 1889; Oxford Classical Texts edition, 1904: now superseded by the edition of R. A. B. Mynors, 1958), E. T. Merrill (1893), W. Kroll (second edition, 1929), and M. Schuster (1949). An increasingly strong preference for the Schuster recension has resulted in my following it religiously in my own work.

The present translation is intended to supplement other currently available translations. My wish has been to bring the modern reader directly into the presence of an intriguing and gifted Roman lyric poet by translating his words and his meaning in equivalent English verses which are unadorned and true to the original in their diction, while disciplined in meter and rhythm. I have tried to mirror Catullus' discipline by using a basically iambic measure throughout and a loose four-stress beat; by approximating the number of lines or verses actually used by Catullus; by rhyming passages most capable of sustaining the effectiveness of rhyme. The strict classical conventions dominating Catullus' poetry of course resist being literally transferred to English poetry. But our own conventions can be applied to the purpose of lyric utterance today as they have been in the past. And a modern translation may attempt not to displace but to restore the poetic vision reflected by the work of its creator.

ROY ARTHUR SWANSON

SELECTED BIBLIOGRAPHY

Translations

Aiken, W. A. (ed.). *The Poems of Catullus*. New York, 1950. (An anthology of verse translations.)

Burton, R. F., and Smithers, L. C. *The Carmina of Caius Valerius Catullus, now first completely Englished into verse and prose*. London, 1894.

Copley, Frank O. *Catullus—The Complete Poetry*. Ann Arbor, 1957. (Verse in the style of E. E. Cummings.)

Gregory, Horace. *The Poems of Catullus*. New York, 1956. (Free verse.)

Kelly, Walter K. *The Poems of Catullus and the Vigil of Venus*. ("Handy Literal Translations.") Harrisburg, Pa., undated. (An erratic but highly entertaining prose translation.)

Lindsay, Jack. *Catullus, the Complete Poems*. London, 1948. (Verse.)

Wright, F. A. *Catullus, the Complete Poems*. London, New York, 1925. (Verse.)

Background

Frank, Tenney. *Catullus and Horace*. New York, 1928.

Havelock, E. A. *The Lyric Genius of Catullus*. Oxford, 1928.

Highet, Gilbert. *Poets in a Landscape*. New York, 1957.

McPeek, J. A. S. *Catullus in Strange and Distant Britain*. ("Harvard Studies in Comparative Literature," Vol. XV.) Cambridge, Mass., 1939.

Richardson, Lawrence. *Poetical Theory in Republican Rome*. New Haven, 1944.

Wheeler, A. L. *Catullus and the Traditions of Ancient Poetry*. Berkeley, 1934.

Wright, F. A. *Three Roman Poets, Plautus, Catullus, Ovid*. London, 1938.

Political and Historical Perspective

Cary, M. *A History of Rome.* London, 1935. 5th ed. 1951.
Cowell, F. R. *Cicero and the Roman Republic.* Baltimore, Md., 1956.
Syme, R. *The Roman Revolution.* Oxford, 1939.
Wilder, Thornton. *The Ides of March.* New York, 1948, 1957.

Classical Tradition

Duckett, Eleanor S. *Catullus in English Poetry.* ("Smith College Classical Studies," No. 6.) Northampton, Mass., 1925.
Harrington, Karl P. *Catullus and His Influence.* Boston, 1923.

NOTE ON THE TEXT

The poems are numbered in accordance with the Latin verses. The number adjoining the last line of each poem indicates the total number of Latin verses in the poem. No verses have been omitted in translation; no poems have been abridged; lacunary dots and asterisks represent actual ellipses in the extant Catullan text (pages 4, 16, 54, 55, 61, 73, 87, 96, 103, 113). Dipyla (pointed brackets) enclose conjectural lines (pages 34, 62).

The translations of poems 2, 3, 5, 7, 8, 43, and 70 were originally published in Volume 52 (1956-1957) of *The Classical Journal*.

R. A. S.

ODI ET AMO

The Complete Poetry of

CATULLUS

1

Cui dono lepidum novum libellum

WHO gets my new slender volume of verse,
    pumice-stone polished? I'll give it to you,
good old Cornelius,[1] who once deigned to think
my trifles were something, when you—
holy Jupiter!—   5
dared to present all time in three tomes,
a labor of learning by one man alone.
So here I submit this bit of a book,
such as it is: and, O Maiden, may you
let it survive for an era or two!   10

2

Passer, deliciae meae puellae

LITTLE sparrow, my lover's love,
    with whom she plays, permits to lie
within her lap to nip her finger,
biting quickly with that bill,
when my shining light of love   5
is pleased to play some little game
to lend her care some tender ease—
her fervor then, I'm sure, must cease—
I should like to play with you
as she, and soothe my troubled heart!   10

1 Cornelius Nepos.

3

2a

Tam gratum est mihi, quam ferunt puellae

.   .   .   .

THAT would be as pleasant as
they say the golden apple was
to the nimble girl [1] who would
have kept her girdle tied for good.   3

3

Lugete, o Veneres Cupidinesque

BE BLUE, every Venus and Cupid
and every sophisticate man;
my sweetheart has lost her sparrow,
her little sparrow has died.
She loved it more than her eyes.   5
It knew her, this mellowy sparrow,
as well as my girl knew her mother;
it never moved from her bosom,
but hopped about here and there
and chirped to its only mistress.   10
   But now it travels the shadows
to the realm from which none return.
Be damned, you damnable shadows
that swallow all beauty for Hell:
you took such a beautiful sparrow.   15
O pitiless crime! pitied sparrow!
For you, now, my sweetheart's eyes
are swollen and red as she cries.   18

[1] Atalanta.

4

Phasellus ille, quem videtis, hospites

MY FRIENDS, that yacht you're looking at
   says it was the swiftest ship,
says no boat of floating beam
could beat it, whether sails or oars
were needed for the clipper's course;   5
denies the Adriatic shores,
so menacing, deny this claim,
or islands of the Cyclades
or Rhodes, renowned, or rugged Thrace,
Propontis, or fierce Pontic bay—   10
where it was foliage before,
as afterward, when whispering
with leaves atop Cytorus' ridge.
   Box-hill Cytorus, the yacht now says
you knew all this, that it stood from birth   15
atop your crest, and wet its oars,
Pontic Amastris, off your shores,
then carried its skipper through scavenger seas,
with larboard or with starboard breeze
or Jupiter's headwind hitting the sheets.   20
Coast gods, it had no need of vows
to you, as it sailed from water break
of sea up to this limpid lake.
   This was its past: but now it rests,   25
grows old in a sequestered sleep
and consecrates itself to you,
Castor, twin, and twin of Castor.[1]   27

1 Pollux.

5

Vivamus, mea Lesbia, atque amemus

L ESBIA, let's live and love
   without one thought for gossip of
the boys grown old and stern.
Suns go down and can return,
but, once put out our own brief light,   5
we sleep through one eternal night.
Give me a thousand, a hundred kisses,
another thousand, a second hundred,
a thousand complete, a hundred repeat;
and when we've many thousand more,   10
we'll scramble them, forget the score
so Malice cannot know how high
the count, and cast its evil eye.   13

6

Flavi, delicias tuas·Catullo

FLAVIUS,
    you'd want to tell Catullus all
about your girl and couldn't be still
unless she were some silly frill.
But shame forbids you to repeat: 5
you're doting on some whore in heat.
Perfumed with wreaths and Syrian oils,
your far from silent sofa spoils
the secret of your prostitute,
denies your nights are destitute;
so dented purse and pillow said,
and quaking of your shaking bed.   10
This silence doesn't hide your game:
your fagged-out flanks would not be lame
without your sorry whoring grind.
So let me in on what you find,   15
both good and bad; I'll call your flame
in facile verse to heaven fame.   17

7

Quaeris, quot mihi basiationes

L ESBIA,
   your question is, How many kisses
should suffice and be supersufficient?
As many as the Libyan sands that lie
on assafoetidal Cyrene,
between Jove's burning oracle and   5
the sepulchral shrine of old Battus
or as many as are the stars that see
men's secret loves in the silent night:
to kiss you with that many kisses
would suffice and be supersufficient   10
for crazy Catullus: the curious
could then never count them and curse us.   12

8

Miser Catulle, desinas ineptire

CATULLUS, poor soul, stop playing the fool;
  write off as loss what you see has been lost.
There used to be days full of sunshine for you,
when you followed the path laid out by your girl.
We loved her as no girl will ever be loved!   5
Those were the days when we had all the fun
which you dearly wanted and she didn't shun;
those were real days full of sunshine for you.
Now, though, she shuns it; so you, useless, don't
chase her and live a poor soul, as she runs: 10
instead, stick it out with a stubborn heart.
So long, girl; Catullus is sticking it out.
He won't look you up; he won't ask you out.
But you will be sorry when none asks you out.
What life—damn you, slut!—is left now for you?   15
Who'll come to you now or think you're a doll?
Whom now will you love or whose claim to be?
Whom will you kiss? Whose lips will you bite?
But you, then, Catullus, be stubborn; sit tight.   19

9

Verani, omnibus e meis amicis

VERANIUS,
  best of all my friends, three
hundred thousand times the best
have you come home to hearth gods,
heart-known brothers, your old
mother? Greatest news! You've come.   5
I'll see you safe and hear you tell
of Spanish persons, places, things,
the way you do; and neck to neck
I'll kiss your mouth and eyes.
Hey, all you wealthy men, I say,   10
who's wealthier than I today?   11

10

Varus me meus ad suos amores

VARUS led me, with nothing to do,
  out of the forum to see his girl,
who seemed, at sudden glance, a whore,
but nice enough and charming too.
Coming here, we made small talk   5
of what Bithynia was like
and whether I'd made money there.
I told the truth and said not even
praetors and cohorts found a way   10
to come back here well-oiled,
especially since our piss-mouth praetor
cared less than a hair for his group.

"But surely," she said, "you managed to get
the native product, a litter man?"   15
To impress the girl as a wealthier type
I said things hadn't gone so bad,
despite the blight the province had,
that I couldn't buy some men, eight straight.   20
(Actually, neither here nor there
had I a man whose neck could trot
the broken leg of an army cot.)
Here she, just like a little trull,
said, "Lend me them for a bit, Catull',   25
I'd like a ride to Serapis' shrine."
"Wait a minute," I told the girl,
"what I just said I had, I mean,
I made a mistake, a friend, you see . . .
Cinna's the one; he got them for me.   30
But his or mine, what's it to me?
I use them as though I'd bought them myself.
But you're a tasteless, troublesome miss
to keep me on my toes like this."   34

11

Furi et Aureli, comites Catulli

FURIUS, Aurelius: friends of Catullus,
    whether he probes the farthest Indies
out where the eastern wave, resounding,
        beats on the shore,

whether he sees soft Arabs, Hyrcanians,   5
Scythian or Parthian archers, or even
sea waters colored by waters of the
        seven-mouthed Nile,

whether he wanders across high Alps,
seeing reminders of mighty Caesar: 10
Gallic Rhine and choppy straits and
        Britons remote—

ready to risk all this and whatever
gods may decide to put in his way:
take and announce to my girl friend a few   15
        words of ill will:

tell her to live with her rakes and be well,
hugging three hundred or more at a time,
loving not one, but, in favor to all,
        pumping their loins;   20

let her not glance at my love as before, who
caused it to fall as a flower falls,
touched at the meadow's edge by a plow
        passing it by.   24

12

Marrucine Asini, manu sinistra

MARRUCINUS Asinius, you use
  your left in dirty way: to lift
the napkins of the guests, not thinking
as they joke and go on drinking.
You're wrong if you think it's funny, you fool!   5
It's a filthy and far from charming act.
Take your brother's word, if you won't take mine;
he'd pay a talent to fence your thefts:
for grace and wit are Pollio's gifts.
So look for a cursing-verse attack   10
or else please send my linen back,
not that it's an expensive brand,
but it's a memento of my friends.
Fabullus and Veranius
sent it from sweaty Saetabis   15
in Spain, a gift to cherish as
I do Verany and Fabullus.   17

13

Cenabis bene, mi Fabulle, apud me

FABULLUS, you will dine with me,
  gods willing, in a day or three,
if you will bring the meal with you,
good and big, a bright girl too,
and wine and salt and lots of laughs.   5
If you bring this, my friend, why, look,
you will dine well: the pocketbook
of your Catullus is well filled
with cobwebs; but, in turn, you will
be unadulterably thrilled
by pleasure, taste—say what you will: 10
I'll have a perfume for you here,
which Love Gods proffered to my dear;
on smelling it, you will propose
that gods above make you all nose.   14

14

Ni te plus oculis meis amarem

IF I didn't love you more than sight,
  genial Calvus, your gift would make
me hate you with Vatinian hate:
what have I done, what have I said
that your plague of poets bruise my head?   5
May the gods malign your client swine
who sent so many works of hacks.
But if, as I suspect, this new
discovery of a gift found you
from Sulla the philologist,
I'm not displeased, but rather eased   10
to see your work not gone to waste.
Great gods, what a gruesome, crooked book!
And you sent it to your Catullus
to make him die in boredom's maze
during Saturnal, our day of days.   15
    No, fraud, you won't get away with this:
at dawn I'll dash to the booksellers' stalls,
buy Caesii, Suffenus, Aquini,
all the poisons in quantities
and repay you with these penalties.   20
    You, meantime, you aches of the age,
move out of here and go back where
you came from, all you poet punks!   23

14a

Si qui forte mearum ineptiarum

WHOEVER of you, by chance, will be
the readers of my trifling works
and lay your fearless hands on me,   3

.   .   .   .

15

Commendo tibi me ac meos amores

AURELIUS,
with my boy-love I give you myself
and make this restrained request:
restraining yourself, keep him pure   5
as you would any hope of your heart.
Not worried by those in the street,
the passersby, here and there,
each bent on his own affair,
I fear only you and your tail,
a terror to any young male.   10
Outside, let it swish whom you wish,
when or where, I don't care, save for him:
an exception which seems to me
duly made with sufficient restraint.
You crook, if your crooked brain   15
does bring you to such a crime
that you tear my life with your snares —
Oh, man, you'll be sorrier more
when I spread your legs and run fish
and radishes through your rear door!   19

16

Pedicabo ego vos et irrumabo

I'LL snag you and gag you, pathic Aurelius;
  I'll gag and snag you, frilly Furius: you,
who both claimed that I too lacked restraint,
from the fact that my verses are rather volupt.
Well, a principled poet might best show restraint,   5
but his verses are free from necessity's taint;
who can deny, then, their spice and salt,
if they're rather volupt and free from restraint
and tickle the prurient impulse in, not,
mind you, boys, but these hairy adults   10
who limber no longer their now hardened loins?
Because you have read of some thousands of kisses,
you think I'm a poor excuse for a man?
I'll snag you and gag you to suit you, my friends.   14

17

O Colonia, quae cupis ponte loedere longo

COLONY, you want to caper on a bridge;
    you're set to dance, but fear the foolish pins
of the bridgelet standing on renovated stakes
will sink and go to sleep in the hollow swamp.
May you get the good long bridge your heart desires;   5
may it even support the Salian rites of Mars,
so long as you let me have this special laugh:
I'd like to see a neighbor of mine go down
head over heels from your bridge and into the mud;
but it has to be in the deepest, deadliest pool
of all the lake and all the stinking swamp.   10
He's the coarsest cad, and he doesn't have the sense
of a two-year-old asleep in a father's arms.
Though he's married a girl in her freshest flower
    and charms
(a girl more delicate than a cuddling kid,   15
more worthy of constant care than the blackest grapes),
he lets her play as she will, not caring a hair;
he won't get up on his own, but lies like a tree
in an Apennine ditch, dropped by a lumberman's ax,
as numb as if he'd never known a wife.   20
My numbskull's so immune to sight and sound,
he can't say who he is or if he is or not.
Now, I want him toppled headlong from the bridge,
to see if it will shake his mental sludge,
his soul left backward in the sluggish slop   25
like an iron mule-shoe stuck in slimy ground.   26

18

Hunc lucum tibi dedico consecroque, Priape

PRIAPUS,[1]
   this grove I dedicate and consecrate to you,
whose living and whose law are known at Lampsacus:
for Hellespontia's coast, more oystery than most
has cities which show special reverence to you.   4

[1] After about 1829, editions of Catullus excluded at least two of the following three "Priapean" poems. Terentianus Maurus, a poet who lived probably during the latter half of the 2nd century A.D., ascribed the first (number 18) to Catullus. The other two (numbers 19 and 20) are undoubtedly spurious. Priapus was a garden god, presumably born to Bacchus and Venus. His effigy, offering protection to gardens both as a guardian spirit and as a scarecrow, was usually of wood and featured a gigantic phallus. The fertility symbol eventually inspired a body of latrine literature.

19

Ego haec, ego arte fabricata rustica

TRAVELER, I, this dry tree, I,
  formed by farmers' art, survey
this little leftward field you see
and the poor owner's cottage and garden,
and check the crimes of thieving hands.   5
I get in spring a colored wreath,
I get in summer reddened grain,
I get the sweet, the green-vined grape,
I get the frost-dried fallen olive.
The tender goat brings milk-filled udders   10
from my pastures into town,
and from my folds the fattened lamb
sends back a hand weighed down with coin.
The soft calf spills its blood before
the temples, while the mother lows.   15
So, traveler, revere this god,
restrain your hand: you'll benefit;
you see this mantool [1] poised for blows.
"Let's see," you say. The bailiff comes:
he'll tear this mantool off and use   20
it as a club; you'll feel his strength.   21

[1] See poem 94.

20

Hunc ego, o iuvenes, locum villulamque palustrem

THIS place, young men, the marsh cottage too,
    thatched with rushes and bundles of twigs,
I, a dry tree, hatchet-hewn,
sustain, so that it gains each year.
This poor hut's owners both revere   5
me as a god, young son and father;
one works diligently to clear
my shrine of weeds and scratchy brambles,
the little one brings me constant gifts.
In Spring I get a colored wreath   10
of early blooms and tender greens;
then violets and milk-white poppies,
pale gourds and sweetly fragrant apples;
then red grapes reared in tendril shade.
Don't tell—but he- and she-goats here   15
have smeared my altar-piece with blood.
Priapus must honor these acts in full
and guard the owner's plants and vines.
So boys, refrain from stealing here.
Our neighbor's rich, and his Priapus   20
is a careless one, so take
from him; this path will lead you there.   21

21

Aureli, pater esuritionum

AURELIUS, you perennial host
     for famine feasts, where food's a ghost,
you'd snag the boy that I love most
and let the whole world know:
with him you laugh and joke and cling   5
beside him, trying everything.
No use: I'll gag you with my tool
before you make me play the fool.
I'd not complain, if you diddled, fed;   10
but you lead the boy around half dead:
with famine and thirst he has to feint.
So stop, while there's credit in restraint,
or you'll end with a gag to blow.   13

22

Suffenus iste, Vare, quem probe nosti

THAT Suffenus, Varus, whom you know so well,
has charm and wit and propriety
and turns out reams of poetry,
ten, or many thousand lines
jotted, not on palimpsest: 5
he has new covers and royal sheets,
new bosses, and red-stained membrane thongs,
straightened with lead, and pumice-smoothed.
But read the stuff, and pretty, proper
Suffenus seems once more a cropper   10
or milker of goats: such a shuddering change.
What should we think? he who seemed just now
a joker, or smoother character,
seems stupider than a stupid hick
as soon as he dabbles in poetry;   15
yet he's never so happy as when he writes,
so great are his pride and self-delights.
But each of us has similar faults;   20
we're each a Suffenus in some respect,
suffering each his personal lack,
blind to the satchel upon his back.   21

23

Furei, cui neque servos est neque arca

FURIUS, you own no slave, no bank,
   no spider, bug, or fire, but own
a dad and second mother, two
whose teeth could grind up even stone.
And life with your old man is good,   5
and with his wife (a block of wood).
No wonder: you're all healthy, your
digestion's good, you have no fear
of fires, heavy losses, or
of crimes, or snares of poison, or   10
of other chance calamity.
But sun- and cold- and famine-worn,
you've bodies drier than a horn
or what has more aridity.
Why shouldn't you be benign and fit?   15
You're free from sweat and free from spit;
your nose is free from snot and slime.
To this fit state add fitter fact,
you're cleaner where your back is cracked
than salt bowls, and it's very clear
you hardly drop ten turds a year,   20
each hard as pebbles or a bean:
your hands can rub them and stay clean.
Count your blessings, Furius, you
shan't spurn or think them all too few—   25
and stop your prayers for sesterces;
you're blest enough with all of these.   27

24

O qui flosculus es Iuventiorum

FLOWER of the Juventii,
    those of today and yesterday
and those of yet another day,
I'd rather you gave Midas' wealth away
to him who owns no slave or bank   5
than let yourself be loved by him.
"A pretty man," you say. He is:
he also owns no slave or bank.
Go, throw my slighted words away:
he has no slave or bank, I say.   10

25

Cinaede Talle, mollior cuniculi capillo

FRILLY Thallus, smoother than bunny fur,
    than goose down, or the lobe of a little ear,
than an old man's listless penis, or spider's web,
yet wilder than the swollen storm, wherein
the goddess goads her sluggish woman scouts: 5
send me my coat, the one you stole, you fool,
my Saetabian scarf and tablets from Thynia,
the ones you're passing off as heir's displays.
Unglue them from your claws and send them back,
or whips will brand your bunny bottom, and   10
write ugly sights upon your tender hands,
    as you strangely heave like a little skiff
    caught on the sea by a wild wind's riff.   13

26

Furi, villula vostra non ad Austri

FURIUS, your villa does not lean
    toward the wind of the South, or the wind
of the West, or Boreas' wind, or Helios';
its lien is a sum of sesterces,
fifteen thousand and two hundred.
O wind of terror, amply thundered!   5

27

Minister vetuli puer Falerni

YOUNG steward of old Falernian wine,
    bring in my cups of drier brine
as Postumia's law has now decreed,
that sot more drunk than a stewed grape seed.
But, Water, woe of wine, go where   5
you will, seek out the stern and square:
I've got the juice of Thyoneus!   7

28
▮▮▮▮▮▮▮▮▮▮

Pisonis comites, cohors inanis

Piso's troopers, coinless group,
   field packs neatly, lightly packed,
Verany, pal, good old Fabull',
what's with you? have you had enough
of foodless frost with that knucklehead?   5
How well did your investment pay?
like mine, which went where praetor led
and left my records in the red?
(O Memmius, you laid me long
and gagged me with your palm-tree prong!)   10
From what I see, you got the same:
stuck with a prick of equal size.
Hereafter, look for high class friends!
   But, Piso, crook, and Memmius, thief,
may gods and goddesses give you grief
for flouting Romulus and Remus!   15

29

Quis hoc potest videre, quis potest pati

WHO can see or support this, unless
  he's an unrestrained lush and a creep:
Mamurra keeps what long-haired Gaul
and remotest Britain kept before.
Will you, pathic Romulus,[1] see and forbear?   5
Will he wander now, superfluous and proud,
through everyone's bed, like a dove of love,
white as a cloud, or like Adonis?
Will you, pathic Romulus, see and forbear?
You're an unrestrained lush and a creep.   10
    Sole commander,[2] was this your role
on the western land's remotest isle,
letting him chew your "bifuckated"
mantool [3] two, three hundred times?
Is this less than left-handed largess?   15
How little did he take out or take in?
To begin, he slashed paternal cash,
then Pontic prizes and those from Spain
known to the gold-bearing Tagus stream;
Gaul and Britain are trembling now.   20
    Why do you favor this fraud, whose only
pitch is to pocket fat patrimonies?
Father- and son-in-law, most vile
smells of the town, is this your case
for shaking down the human race?   24

1 Julius Caesar is meant.
2 Again, Julius Caesar is meant.
3 See poem 94.

30

Alfene immemor atque unanimis false sodalibus

ALFENUS, forgetful and false to all your friends,
   liar, quick to delude and deceive me now,
have you no heart, hard-head, for your old pal?
Well, the gods don't like the dirty work of sneaks;
but you don't care, you leave me in the lurch.   5
Hell, what can men do; say, whom can they trust?
You really made me sell my soul, you crook,
leading me to a love you said was sure.
You back out now and let the winds and clouds
blow all your worthless words and deeds away.   10
If you forget, the gods will not, nor Trust,
who'll later make you rue your gruesome crust.   12

31

Paene insularum, Sirmio, insularumque

SIRMIO,
   eyelet of isles and almost-islands
carried by Neptune of Liquid Lakes
or the other Neptune, of Open Sea,
how pleasant, how perfect to see you again
in safety; it's hard to believe that I've left
Bithynia's plains and Thynia behind!   5
   O what is better than unbottled cares
when the mind is unburdened and we come home,
weary of work and wandering,
to find our rest in the bed we've missed?   10
This makes up for all our work.
   Hello, you lovely Sirmio;
delight in your landlord; all you waves
of the Lydian lake, likewise delight:
laugh, all you laughs of local birth!   14

32

Amabo, mea dulcis Ipsitilla

PLEASE, Ipsitilla, sugar,
    my doll, kid, baby, please
tell me to come this afternoon;
contribute to my ease
by letting no one lock your door,   5
by staying where you are; what's more,
get set to soothe me, as I choose,
with nine uninterrupted screws.
Whatever gives, don't make me wait:
I'm lying, filled with all I ate,   10
watching my tunic stand up straight.   11

33

O furum optime balneariorum

YOU'RE the best of bathhouse burglars,
    Vibennius, you and your pathic son
(the father flaunts a fouler hand,
the son a greedier ass):
why don't you prowl perverted lands   5
as exiles, where the people know
the father's thefts, and, son, where you
can penny-vend your hairy clefts.   8

34

Dianae sumus in fide

WE ARE in Diana's trust,
    girls and untouched boys:
⟨untouched boys and girls,⟩
    let us sing Diana.

Latonia, mighty progeny   5
of mighty Jupiter,
your mother laid you down
    beside the Delian olive

to be thereby the queen of hills,
the queen of greening woods,   10
the queen of hidden groves
    and queen of sounding streams.

Women lost in labor pains
call you Lucina Juno,
powerful Trivia, known as Luna   15
    by your borrowed brilliance.

Goddess measuring out the year
with a menstrual career,
you fill the farmers' rustic homes
    with fruits heaped to the roofs.   20

Whatever name you like the best,
be blest in it, sustain the race
of Romulus with precious help,
    your customary grace.   24

35

Poetae tenero, meo sodali

PAPER,[1] I'd like you to tell my friend,
   the budding poet, Caecilius, to
leave Novum Comum, its Larian shore,
and come to Verona to hear three or four   5
ideas from one who is his friend and mine.

If wise, he would run all the way, although
recalled by his beautiful girl, who'll throw
both arms to his neck, say her thousandth no
when he moves to go. She it is, if it's so,   10
who is lost in her violent love for him.

Since he read her the *Lady of Dindymus*,
a work he's begun, the fires have fed
on the marrow bed of the poor girl's bones.   15
Girl, more gifted than Sappho's muse,
you're excused; for Caecilius indeed has done
well with the *Cybele* he has—begun.   18

1 I have attempted to render this translation in keeping with the obser-
vations made by Prof. Frank O. Copley in his article, "Catullus, 35"
(*American Journal of Philology*, April, 1953, pp. 149-160). Prof. Copley
writes: "Caecilius has sent Catullus a copy of his *Magna Mater*, giving
him the impression that he considers it a finished job, ready for publi-
cation. Catullus reads it, and becomes concerned. The poem shows
great promise, but if it is released in its present form, it will be bound
to bring down the critics on Caecilius' head . . . . He invites Caecilius
to come to see him . . . . But Caecilius misses the point of the invita-
tion, and replies that he can't come, since he is at the moment ab-
sorbed in a love affair. Disappointed, too, that he had not received
praise for his work, he reiterates his opinion that it is ready for publi-
cation Now Catullus writes [poem] 35, telling Caecilius that he really
must come . . . ; he has certain 'thoughts' which he wants Caecilius to
hear. His poem is excellent—so good, in fact, that the reading of it
must have been the cause of that tremendous passion which Caecilius'

36

Annales Volusi, cacata carta

VOLUSIAN annals, turd-bound tomes,
     help my sweetheart keep a vow:
she swore to Cupid and blessed Venus
that, if I were restored to her
and ceased to brandish iamb spears,   5
she'd give the limping god [1] a book
of the lousiest poet's choicest verse
to be burned in a fire of unfortunate wood.
She sees in this the worst stuff yet
that, even in joke, the gods could get.   10
    Now, goddess, born in the deep blue sea,
living in holy Idalium
and on the open Urian plains,
in reedy Cnidus and Ancona,
Amathus, Golgos, Dyrrachium,
the tavern of the Adriatic;   15
receive and accept the vow, unless
you think it uncharming and lusterless.
But you, meantime, with your grace of barns
and latrines, leap into flaming homes,
Volusian annals, turd-bound tomes!   20

---

lady has conceived for him . . . . She is a girl of real taste! But he
must come anyway; his work is charming but—unfinished . . . ." In
this way Prof. Copley stresses Catullus' placement of the key thought,
the unifying idea, at the dramatic end of the poem.
    1 Vulcan.

37

Salax taberna vosque contubernales

BARFLIES with your slimy tavern,
nine posts from the skull-capped brothers,[1]
you think that you alone have mantools,[2]
that you alone can screw the girls
and label others goat-foul fools?   5
Or do you sit in silly bliss
because you are two hundred strong
and think perhaps I wouldn't dare
to gag two hundred, chair to chair?
You're wrong: I'll use you, dull and blunt,
to scribble up every tavern front!   10
My girl, who runs from my embrace,
loved, as none will ever be loved,
by me, who fought fierce wars for her,
frequents your place and takes the love
of all of you, the high-born crew   15
and all the punks and alley slew;
but, worst of all, Egnatius, you,
you long-haired son of bunny-Spain,
whose bushy beard attracts the Miss,
and teeth brushed white with Spanish piss.   20

[1] Castor and Pollux.
[2] See poem 94.

38

Malest, Cornifici, tuo Catullo

CORNIFICIUS, Catullus, your friend, is sick;
   by Hercules, man, mighty sick, bad off
and getting worse every day and hour.
And what condolence have you given him,
as easy a little thing as that?   5
I'm irked with you. My love nets this?
Some little word of condolence—please:
more sad than the tears of Simonides.   8

39

Egnatius, quod candidos habet dentes

BECAUSE Egnatius has white teeth, he smiles
without a stop. And should it come to trials
where lawyers move the court to tears, he smiles.
Suppose a mother mourns her only son,   5
he smiles. Whatever it is, whatever he's done,
wherever it is, he smiles. It's a disease,
not elegance, I think, nor does it please.
So, good Egnatius, I must give you warning,
were you a Roman, Sabine, Tiburtine,   10
or frugal Umbrian, or fat Etruscan,
or dark Lanuvian with big buck teeth,
or Transpadane—to bring my people in—
or one of any group which cleans its teeth
with water, constant smiles would still displease: 15
nothing's as far from tact as tactless grins.
But you're from Spain, and Spain's the spot
where teeth are scrubbed and red gums rubbed with what
is pissed the night before into a pot,
so that your tooth tells by its higher shine   20
how much you've drunk the dregs of bedroom wine.   21

40

Quaenam te mala mens, miselle Ravide

RAVIDUS, poor fool,
    what malady now moves
you headlong into my iambics?
What deity, who plans your fall,
is stirring up this stupid brawl?
Is it to be the talk of town   5
you want, or is your hope renown?
You'll get it, with a lot of grief,
trying to love my love, you thief!   7

41

Ameana, puella defututa

AMEANA, a slit-shot frail,
    with a nose as cruddy as her tail,
playmate of playboy Formian,
duns me, not *one* grand, but *ten!*
Neighbors, whom she calls her proctors,   5
call her friends and call her doctors!
She's not all there, nor does she care
to check her class in a looking glass.   8

42

Adeste, hendecasyllabi, quot estis

COME, hendecasyllabics, come,
  all, from all over, come one and all!
The dirty tart thinks I'm a joke
and says that she will not give back
your tablets—tolerate that tripe!   5
Let's track her down and call them back.
    You ask her name? Why, she's the dame
who swings her hips, her smutty lips
laughing like a Gallic whelp: 10
"Stinking tart, return the notes,
return, you stinking tart, the notes!"
    No dice? O slop, you whorehouse curse
or what could be a damned sight worse!
But this must not be thought enough.   15
At least, if it does nothing else,
let's turn her poker dogface red.
Shout once again, more loudly now:
"Stinking tart, return the notes,
return, you stinking tart, the notes!"   20
    But it's no good; she can't be budged.
We'll have to try a new approach
to see if you can get more done:
"Virgin pure, return the notes!"   24

43

Salve, nec minimo puella naso

HELLO, girl—you, with the *un*short nose,
    with the *un*fine foot and the *un*dark eyes,
the *un*long fingers and the *un*dry mouth,
and the not too elegant *un*clean tongue,
playmate of playboy Formian.   5
Do they call you a beauty in nearer Gaul?
Is my Lesbia there compared to you?
O the world is senseless and witless too!   8

44

O funde noster, seu Sabine seu Tiburs

O FARM of mine, whether you're Tibur's or Sabine
   (for those who leave Catullus' heart untorn assert
you're Tiburtine, but those who don't say you're Sabine);
but whether you're Sabine or, better, Tiburtine,   5
in your suburban house I gladly took my rest,
dislodged a vicious cold that settled in my chest—
my stomach gave the thing to me, as I deserved,
when I gulped luscious banquets sumptuously served.
You see, while I took time to be a Sestian guest,   10
I read his speech against the claimant Antius,
full of pestilence and fully poisonous.
At this, an icy chill and repetitious cough
shook me, until I fled into your sanctuary
to find my health again with rest and stimulants.   15
    And so, refreshed, I here extend great thanks to you
because you've not exacted for my guilt its due.
And I am not avoiding Sestius' wretched works;
just let them give, not me, the cold and cough that
       jerks,   20
but him, whose invitations mean more trash to read.   21

45

Acmen Septimius suos amores

HOLDING his sweetheart in his lap,
Septimius said, "My Acme, if
I do not love you desperately
nor look to love eternally
as much as mortal man can love,   5
why, let me meet a green-eyed beast
in Libya or India's flame."
At this, Love sneezed from left to right,
repeating his approval rite.

Acme gently turned her head   10
and kissed her sweetheart's drunken eyes
with lips rose-red, and then she said,
"Septimillus, my life, let's live
for this one lord alone as long   15
as fire melts my mellow marrow,
mounting in mightier flames of love."
At this, Love sneezed from left to right,
repeating his approval rite.

Progressing from good auspices,
they smother each other in equal love.   20
Septimius loves his Acme more
than Syria, Britain, and all between,
while Acme finds Septimius source
of all delights and pleasantries.
Were mortals ever happier,   25
or passion more auspicious?   26

46

Iam ver egelidos refert tepores

N ow Spring is bringing gentle sun
and heaven's equinoctial roar
dies down before the pleasant western breeze.
The Phrygian fields, Catullus, are no more:
behind are hot Nicaea's soil and trees.   5
To Asia's brilliant cities let us run!
The hasty heart knows wanderlust;
the anxious legs become robust.
Our paths diverge: old troupe, goodbye.
Our distant home for each must lie   10
beneath each journey's other sky.   11

47

Porci et Socration, duae sinistrae

S OCRATION and Porky, Piso's thugs,
famine scabs of the world, are you
favored by that Priapus above
Fabullus and my Verany-O?
Does the circumcised Priapus serve
you sumptuous daily drinks and eats?   5
my friends go begging in the streets?   7

48

Mellitos oculos tuos, Iuventi

SHOULD someone, dear Juventius, let
    me kiss your honeyed eyes, I bet
I'd kiss three hundred thousand times,
nor yet seem satisfied until
our kisses were more dense than beards   5
of grain dried on a harvest hill.   6

49

Disertissime Romuli nepotum

OF ALL the line of Romulus,
    you, my Marcus Tullius,[1]
are more articulate by far
than all who were, will be, or are:
Catullus thanks you very much,
Catullus, poet worst of all,   5
as much the poet worst of all
as you're the lawyer best of all.   7

[1] Cicero.

50

Hesterno, Licini, die otiosi

LICINIUS,
   during our lazy yesterday
we gave my tablets quite a play
in our sophisticated way.
Each of us fooled around in verse,
dabbling in metrics to fill a line,   5
changing off with laughs and wine.
   Licinius, I left your place,
so charged with all your grins and grace
that food provided me no prize
and sleep could not control my eyes,   10
and wildly tossed in bed all night
just waiting for the morning light,
to see and be with you again.
But once my limbs gave out in bed,
I wrote this poem for you, half-dead,   15
to let you know of my chagrin.
   Now, don't presume to spurn my prayers,
I beg you, jewel of my brain,
or Nemesis will ask your pain.   20
She's a goddess and she's strong:
I tell you, man, don't do her wrong.   21

51

Ille mi par esse deo videtur

THAT fellow seems the same as a god,
    seems, if I may, to excel the gods,
as he sits beside you and at one time
        watches and hears you

laughing gently; and I am deprived   5
of my senses by this, for seeing you once,
Lesbia, nothing remains of my voice,
        nothing at all;

but my tongue grows numb, a subtle flame
flows through my limbs, my ears are ringing   10
with sounds of their own, my eyes are covered
        by veils of night.

Sloth, Catullus, for you, is loss,
sloth informs you to excess,
sloth before has ruined kings   15
        and wealthy cities.   16

52

Quid est, Catulle? quid moraris emori?

CATULLUS, why not call it quits?
    In office itchy Nonius sits.
Vatinius, consul, counterfeits.
Catullus, why not call it quits?   4

53

Risi nescioquem modo e corona

JUST now I laughed at a listener,
   who, when my Calvus had neatly disclosed
the charges against Vatinius,
said, inspired, his hands in a fidget,
"My god, what an eloquent midget!"   5

54

Otonis caput oppido est pusillum

CAESAR,
   Otto's[1] head is mighty dinky,
Harry's[2] barnyard legs half-washed,
Libo's sneaky fart is stinky;
if all of these do not disgust
you, then Sufficius will, I trust,
that ancient retread, stuffed with lust—   5
my level lines will lend you pique
again, commander, so unique.   7

---

[1] *Oto*, Ot(h)o.
[2] *Herius.* Actually the Latin *Arrius* (see poem 84) is more approximate to "Harry."

55

Oramus, si forte non molestum est

U NLESS it's going much too far,
please tell me where your shadows are.
In Circus, Little Field, and all
the stalls of books I've looked for you,
in mighty Jove's clean temple, too.   5
In Pompey's portico, my friend,
I asked the chicks around the place,
all those, at least, who kept straight face,
demanding you with words like this:
"My Camisole,[1] you maudlin miss!"   10
One said, as she laid bare her slips,
"Here's one I've hid on rosy pips."
It's Hercules' work to get you then,
flying so high, my friend, you wren?
Tell me where you're going to be,   15
speak up, some daylight, please, for me.
You're not the slave of milk-white girls?
Keep your tongue locked up all day,
you'll throw love's every gift away:
Venus' delight is wordy speech.   20
Or, keep your love behind a gate
so long as I participate.   22

[1] The name of Catullus' elusive friend is *Camerius*. The name appears in the poem in the accusative case, i.e., *Camerium*. Prof. Frank O. Copley ("Catullus 55, 9-14," *American Journal of Philology*, LXXIII [1952], 295-7) explains that a neuter noun, *camerium,* can be defined in Latin by *zonula* (girdle). The name *Camerius* would then be the subject of a pun. Prof. Copley's interpretation, it seems to me, makes the poem entirely clear. Attempting to render the pun, I have translated *Camerius* by *Camisole.*

56

O rem ridiculam, Cato, et iocosam

HEY, Cato, here's a joke, which you
   might like to hear and laugh at too.
Laugh it up, if you like Catullus:
this is a gasser to turn you blue.
I caught a kid who was shoving it to   5
a little girl; by Dione, here
I ran him through, with my hard for spear.   7

57

Pulcre convenit improbis cinaedis

THOSE frilly lechers make a lively pair,
   Mamurra and the pathic Caesar there.
No wonder, one at Formia and one
at Rome, they've broken out in equal lots
of spots that stay and will not be rubbed off: 5
each has a little learning in his head,
they're both diseased and share a little bed,
show equal greed in gross adultery,
of girls they're friendly rivals, fair and square:
those frilly lechers make a lively pair.   10

58

Caeli, Lesbia nostra, Lesbia illa

CAELIUS, that Lesbia, my woman,
    that—that Lesbia, whom once I, Catullus,
loved above himself and closest cronies,
now rubs up the grandsons of lordly Remus
on the corners and in the narrow alleys.   5

58a

Non custos si fingar ille Cretum

NOT if I were that guard of Crete [1]
    nor flew with Pegasus as seat,
nor ran with Perseus' winged feet
as fast as Ladas, not if I
had Rhesus' snow-swift horses by;
add feather-footed flight to these,   5
the speeds of winds require, please;
suppose you gave them all to me
my Camisole,[2] though I might be
bone-weary, weak, and near my end,
I'd still chase after you, my friend.   10

1 Talos, a brass man created by Vulcan.
2 See poem 55.

59

Bononiensis Rufa Rufulum fellat

RUFUS [1] gets sucked by Bononian Rufa,
    Menenius' wife, whom you've often seen
in cemeteries, snitching pyre-food,
chasing bread that bobbles from the fire,
cornholed by the half-shaved corpse cremator.   5

60

Num te leaena montibus Libystinis

A LIBYAN mountain lioness bore you, no?
    or Scylla barking from her bottom loins?
So adamant and savage is your soul
that you would sneer at those who beg for help
at ruin's edge, ach, heart too like a beast!   5

[1] Rufulus.

61

Collis o Heliconiei

O CULTOR of Helicon,
    born of Urania,
you take to a husband
a tender virgin.
O Hymenaeus Hymen
O Hymen Hymenaeus,   5

beflower your brows with
sweet marjoram blossoms,
take the red veil and
come happily here, white
foot yellow-sandaled,   10

aroused by this joyful day,
singing with silver voice
songs for the wedding, beat
earth with your feet, with your
hand shake the torch!   15

For Vinia—as Venus,
Idalium's protectress,
approached Phrygia's judge—
comes, good, with good omen,
in marriage to Manlius,   20

shining like myrtle
on Asia's branched blooms,
which divine Hamadryades
nourish with dew
in private delight.   25

Come then this way,
leave the Thespian cliff,
its Aonian caves,
which the nymph Aganippe
cools with clear waters,   30

and call home the mistress,
who yearns for her man;
love-twine her heart
as the ivy vine, errant,
twines tightly its tree.   35

And, pure virgins, to whom
a like day will come,
come likewise, in rhythm
chant, "O Hymenaeus Hymen,
O Hymen Hymenaeus,"   40

so the guide of good Venus,
good love's conjugator,
will more willingly hear
his call to his duty
and direct his way here.   45

What god ought lovers
more to petition?
Whom in the heavens ought
men more to worship?
O Hymenaeus Hymen,
O Hymen Hymenaeus.   50

A father in fear calls
on you, for whom virgins
undo their small girdles,
at whom a scared bridegroom,
with yearning ear, grasps.   55

From her mother's lap you
transfer to hands of
fierce youth the flowering
girl, O Hymenaeus Hymen,
O Hymen Hymenaeus.   60

Venus without you
can reap no advantage
approved by opinion, but
can if you're willing,
incomparable god.   65

No house without you
can offer an heir, no
parent know lineage, but
can if you're willing,
incomparable god.   70

No land without your
rites could protect
its boundaries, but
could were you willing,
incomparable god.   75

Barriers, unbar! The maiden
is here. Do you mark how the
fires shake their bright hairs?
·   ·   ·   ·   ·   ·   ·
·   ·   ·   ·   ·   ·   ·   80

·   ·   ·   ·   ·   ·   ·
·   ·   ·   ·   ·   ·   ·
Maiden restraint retards:
in attendance to which she weeps
the more, for she must depart.   85

Don't cry, Aurunculeia,
there is no danger that
any more beautiful girl
will ever see bright day
emerging from Ocean.   90

In the varied garden
of a monied master,
so stands a hyacinth:
but day wanes as you wait:
come on, you young bride.   95

Come on, you young bride,
it's all right now;
hear us and mark how
fires shake golden hairs:
come on, you young bride.   100

Your man, never fickle
or, prone to adultery,
looking for lust, won't
wish to sleep parted
from your tender breasts.   105

As the clinging vine folds
itself about trees,
so will your embrace
enfold him. But day wanes:
come on, you young bride.   110

O couch, which to all
.   .   .   .   .   .
.   .   .   .   .   .
.   .   .   .   .   .
by the bed's white foot,   115

what pleasure's afoot
for your lord in dim
night or high noon;
what delight! But day wanes:
come on, you young bride.   120

Boys, raise the torches:
I see the red veil.
Come, sing in rhythm,
"Yo Hymen Hymenaeus yo,
yo Hymen Hymenaeus."   125

Unsilence the dirty
fescennine jokes,
and bed-boy, now losing
the master's love, keep
no nuts from the boys.   130

Give nuts to the boys,
idle bed-boy, you've played
with nuts long enough:
yield to Thalassius.
Hey, bed-boy, the nuts!   135

No farm foremen's wives
for you, bed-boy, till now:
today the beautician is
shaving your face. Oh,
poor bed-boy, the nuts!   140

Bridegroom, they say you
will not abstain from
sweet slaves: but abstain!
Yo Hymen Hymenaeus yo,
yo Hymen Hymenaeus.   145

We know the permissible
pleasures you've known,
but they're not for a groom.
Yo Hymen Hymenaeus yo,
yo Hymen Hymenaeus.   150

And, bride, do not keep
from your man what he wants,
or he'll know where to go.
Yo Hymen Hymenaeus yo,
yo Hymen Hymenaeus.   155

Note your man's house,
how wealthy and strong:
long let it serve you
(yo Hymen Hymenaeus yo,
yo Hymen Hymenaeus),   160

until grey old age,
nodding quivering head
grants all things to all.
Yo Hymen Hymenaeus yo,
yo Hymen Hymenaeus.   165

Set your fine feet across
the threshold for luck, and go
under the polished door!
Yo Hymen Hymenaeus yo,
yo Hymen Hymenaeus.   170

Look, on the purple couch,
lying alone, your lord
longs wholly for you!
Yo Hymen Hymenaeus yo,
yo Hymen Hymenaeus.   175

Deep burns his love
in his breast, not less
than yours does, but deeper.
Yo Hymen Hymenaeus yo,
yo Hymen Hymenaeus.   180

Release the maid's arm
so smooth and so small, boy:
let her find her man's bed.
Yo Hymen Hymenaeus yo,
yo Hymen Hymenaeus.   185

You women, well known
to husbands now aged,
arrange the maid!
Yo Hymen Hymenaeus yo,
yo Hymen Hymenaeus.   190

Groom, you may come, your
wife's in her wedding bed,
her face is aglow
like white maidenflower
or yellow poppy.   195

But, god help me, groom,
you're just as attractive,
nor did Venus neglect you.
But day wanes, so go,
don't hesitate so.   200

You've not delayed long.
Now you come. May good Venus
assist you, you want
no secret love, what
you want you want right.   205

Let him who would number
your thousandfold pleasures
number beforehand
Africa's sands and
the candent stars.   210

Play as you please and
bear children; for such
an old name should never
lose heirs, but should ever
engender its line.   215

A tiny Torquatus
in his mother's lap,
his little lips grinning,
his soft hands reaching
for daddy: my wish.   220

May he be like Manlius;
and in his face,
strange to no strangers,
easily known, may his mother's
faithfulness be shown.   225

Praise gained from his mother
will enhance his clan
as that from Penelope,
greatest of mothers,
remains with Telemachus.   230

Close the doors, virgins:
we've played enough.
Live well, newlyweds,
fulfill the fabric
of vigorous youth.   235

62

Vesper adest: iuvenes, consurgite! Vesper Olympo

Boys:

HERE is the Evening Star, young men! It brings
Olympus at last its long awaited light.
Now is the time to rise and resign rich meals:
the Maid will come, the wedding song be sung.
    Hymen o Hymenaeus, come Hymen o Hymenaeus!   5

Girls:

Single girls, do you see the boys? Rise up!
The Evening Star displays Oetaean flames.
All right: do you see how swiftly they've sprung forth?
not casually: they'll sing what you're to surpass.
    Hymen o Hymenaeus, come Hymen o Hymenaeus!   10

Boys:

Fellows, no facile prize is prepared for us:
see how the single girls want careful plans!
They don't plan uselessly: they've something good;
no wonder, when they work with single mind.
With us, our minds are strangers to our ears;   15
so we'll lose rightly: victory loves care.
So now, at least pay some attention, please!
They'll soon begin to chant; we'll have to answer.
    Hymen o Hymenaeus, come Hymen o Hymenaeus!

Girls:

Hesperus, what heaven flame is worse?   20
You tear a daughter from her mother's arms,
can tear her, clinging, from a mother's arms
and give the virgin to a hot young man.
What enemies do worse in captured towns?
    Hymen o Hymenaeus, come Hymen o Hymenaeus!   25

Boys:

Hesperus, what heaven flame's more pleasing?
You, with your flame, sustain the wedding vows
which men and future in-laws made before
but did not carry out before you burned.
What gift of gods excels that happy hour?   30
    Hymen o Hymenaeus, come Hymen o Hymenaeus!

Girls:

Hesperus has taken one of us.

      *   *   *   *

Boys:

When you come out, the guard is always alert.
Thieves [1] hide by night, but often in return
you catch them, Hesperus, renamed Dawn Star.   35
It pleases virgins to blame you with false complaint.
What if they blame what their secret hearts desire?
    Hymen o Hymenaeus, come Hymen o Hymenaeus!

Girls:

As the flower grows, concealed by garden walls,
unknown to herds, uprooted by no plow,   40
nursed and trained by breezes, soil, and rain . . .
and many boys and girls desire it;
but once it's faded, after being plucked,
not any boys or girls desire it:
just so the girl, who's dear while she's untouched,   45
when once, her body stained, she's lost her flower,
displeases boys and is not dear to girls.
    Hymen o Hymenaeus, come Hymen o Hymenaeus!

---

[1] I.e., lovers.

Boys:

As the vine which grows unwed in barren fields,
which never rises and never rears rich grapes,   50
but bends its tender mass beneath its weight
and touches its topmost shoot with lowest root,
is scorned by farmers and young bucks alike,
but joined, by chance, and married to an elm
is sought by farmers and young bucks alike: 55
just so the girl, will, untouched, age unsought;
but if, when time is ripe, she takes a mate,
he loves her more, there's less parental hate.
⟨Hymen o Hymenaeus, come Hymen o Hymenaeus!⟩

Girls and Boys:

So do not fight with such a husband, girl!   60
It's wrong to fight; your father gave him you,
your mother, too; you must obey them both.
Virginity is not entirely yours:
one third your father owns, one third your mother,
one third alone is yours: don't fight with two   65
who've sold a son-in-law their rights to you.
Hymen o Hymenaeus, come Hymen o Hymenaeus!   67

63

Super alta vectus Attis celeri rate maria

SWIFT-SHIPPED Attis, having sailed steep seas,
       touched Phrygia's forest with frantic foot
and entered the goddess's forested shades,
where, prodded, rabid, unsettled in mind,
he hacked off the hang of his loins with flint.   5
And so, as he saw his limbs left unmanned
and his fresh blood spotting the soil of the land,
her swift snowy hands seized tambours, light,
used, Cybele, Mother, in rites for you,
soft-handedly shook the hollow hide   10
and, shaking, she sang to her sharers these songs:
      "Come, Gallae, together to Cybele's groves,
come, roaming droves of Dindymene, who,
like refugees looking for foreign lands,
following my lead as loyal friends,   15
have suffered swift sea and the deadly deeps
and unmanned your bodies with loathing for love,
elate with mad motion the heart of the Lady,
unseat slow delay from your minds; come all
to Cybele's Phrygian home and groves,   20
where the cymbals scream, where the tambours sound,
the Phrygian flutist flares curved reed,
where ivyclothed Maenads wave wild heads,
where they pierce their rites with ululation,
where the goddess's wandering band would go,   25
to where we'd best hurry with hasty dance."
      As Attis, the "woman," so sang to her sharers,
the band wailed abruptly with wavering tongues,
light tambour re-echoes and cymbals clang,

to green Ida quickly the chorus cavorts.   30
Mad Attis goes gasping, dancing to death,
followed by tambours, through darkened groves,
like an untamed heifer avoiding the yoke:
the swift Gallae follow their fleetfooted guide.
When, weary, they come to Cybele's home,   35
from excessive exertion they sleep unfed.
Listless sleep idles upon their eyes;
their frantic fury abates in rest.
    When the golden sun with shining eyes
surveyed white air, hard earth, wild sea,   40
and shattered night shadows with stamping steeds,
sleep swiftly abandoned awakened Attis,
whom Pasithea took to her trembling breast.
From the vantage of rest without wild rage
Attis went over her deeds in her heart,   45
saw lucidly where and without what she'd be,
and, seething in soul, sought the shore once more.
There, seeing vast seas with her tearfilled eyes,
distressed, she addressed her native land:
    "My land O my creatress, my land O my womb,   50
I left you as runaway slaves leave lords
and came, poor me, to the groves of Ida,
to settle in snow and savagely go
to the icy dens, all the lairs of beasts:
where shall I suppose you now lie, my land?   55
My eye wants to send its glance your way,
while my mind rests briefly from wild unbalance.
Will I wander these woods away from my home,
my land, possessions, my parents and friends,
from stadium, gym, palaestra and forum?   60
My sad sad soul must complain and complain!
What kind of a form have I not gone through?
I, woman, was man, young man and boy,

I was pride of the gym, a wrestling wonder:
my doors were crowded, my doorsill warm,   65
my house was wreathed with flowery garlands
when I had to leave my bed at dawn.
Shall I cater to gods, be Cybele's slave?
Shall I remain minus a part of myself?
Shall I be a Maenad or emasculate male?
Shall I cherish land wrapped in Green Ida's snow?   70
Shall I live under lofty ridges of Phrygia
with sylvan deer, with woodranging boar?
Already I'm sorry for what I have done."
   When the sound which rose from her red lips reached
the gods' doubled ears with announcements anew,   75
then Cybele freed her lions from their yoke
and, pricking the curse of the herd, so spoke:
   "Up, fierce one, infuse this fellow with frenzy,
force him back to the forest in a fit of fury,
since he feels, too freely, he must flee my rule.   80
Thrash your back with your tail, let the
whole locale resound with your roars,
toss your tawny mane with your muscular neck!"
   So Cybele menaced, and yielded the yoke.
The beast spurs its speed, builds its spirit up,   85
runs, roars and tramps down small trees in its way.
When it neared the damps of the whitening shore
and noted soft Attis hard by the surf,
it attacks: Attis, maddened, fled into the woods.
There *he* lived as bonds*maid* all of his life.   90
   Good goddess, great Cybele, grand lady of Dindymus,
keep your fury, my lady, away from my home:
drive others to madness, drive others insane!   93

64

Peliaco quondam prognatae vertice pinus

PINES once sprung from Pelion's crest
    are said to have navied Neptune's waves
to Phasian flows, Aeetean fronts,
when chosen youth, the Argive oak,
wishing to bring the Golden Fleece   5
from Colchis, dared to cross the sea
and slap cerulean waves with firs.
The goddess of soaring citadels [1]
fashioned, Herself, the flying car,
conjoining pines with curving keel: 10
the first ship Amphitrite knew.
As soon as its beak bit the windy sea
and the oar-wound waters whitened with foam,
from the whitened sea wild faces emerged,
marine Nereids agape at the sight.   15
On that day alone did human eyes
view nymphs of the sea arising nude
from the foamy waves, with breasts exposed.
Then Thetis, they say, fired Peleus' love,
then Thetis agreed to wed mortal man,   20
then Thetis's father, Himself, blessed the match.
O heroes born in time's finest age,
all hail! and, heavenly progeny,
men nobly mothered, all hail again!   23b
You, in my song, I shall often address,
and you, O pillar of Thessaly, Peleus,   25
so greatly honored with torches of pine,
whose bride the Father of Gods endowed,

1 Athena.

Jupiter Himself, who yielded his love.
Did Thetis, the prettiest Nereid take:
did Tethys and Ocean, the world-circling sea,
offer their grandchild in marriage to: you?   30
   The great day came in passing time;
all Thessaly thronged to this home to fill
the court of the king with a joyous crowd:
giving gifts to Peleus, smiling their joy.
Cieros: deserted, and Phthiotican Tempe,   35
Crannon's homes, and the walls of Larissa;
men come to Pharsalia, they crowd its halls.
Steers' necks soften: none tills the soil;
no curved rakes clear lowlying vines;
no bull tows the plow through the glebe;   40
no hook prunes the leaves spreading shade;
rust flakes form on forgotten plows.
But the opulent palace of Peleus shines
with silver and gold where its halls recede.
Thrones' ivory glistens and goblets gleam,   45
the great house is charmed by regal wealth.
The nuptial couch of the goddess, placed
in the palace midst, inlaid with tusk,
is covered with cloth all colored rose-red
with dye which the purple shell provides.

   This varied vestment shows venerable men   50
and the virtues of heroes with marvelous art:
Gazing from Naxos' wave-sounding shore,
Ariadne sees Theseus sail his swift ship
and bears in her heart an unbridled rage,
unable as yet to believe what she sees,   55
as just now aroused from treacherous sleep
she finds herself left on lonely sand.
Faithless, the youthful fugitive sails,
leaving vain vows to the fickle wind.

Like a Bacchante of stone in seaweed, she,   60
Minos' daughter, with saddened eyes,
sees him far off from her billows of grief;
no simple band binds her blond hair;
no veiling gown hides her bare breasts,
no cincture guards their nipples from harm: 65
the garments, dropped from her body, were
washed by the waves of salt at her feet.
Heedless of band and flowing gown,
caring for you wholeheartedly,
Theseus, she hovered with harried mind.   70
Poor girl, within whose breast Love stormed
to sow with ceaseless sorrows griefs
that sting and prick, when Theseus, fierce,
forsook the curved Piraean shores
and came to Crete, Gortynian home
of Minos, king by wrongful rule.   75
    They say that Cecrops' city once,
forced to atone for Androgeos slain,
forbore and fed the Minotaur
its finest boys and fairest girls.   80
Theseus, who saw his city maimed,
chose, for Athens' sake, to yield
his life, forestalling, by such death
for Crete, Cecropian funerals.
And so he sailed with gentle winds
to mighty Minos' lofty home.   85
And there the princess cast love's eye
on him, she whom a maiden's bed
embraced in soft maternity,
breathing forth clean maiden scents
as sweet as myrtles which Eurotas
brings upon its banks, or blooms   90
brought out by vernal air. Her eyes

burned bright nor left his form before
love's flame consumed her very bones.
Good Cupid, stirring savage rage
with wicked heart, commingling woe   95
and human joy, and Venus, queen
of green Idalium, Golgos too,
on what tremendous floods you threw
this girl whose burning heart desired
the stranger with the yellow hair!
How great her fears in fainting heart,
her face more pale than yellow gold,   100
when Theseus wished to wage his war
against the beast for death or praise!
Her prayers, addressed with lips compressed,
vowed gifts, god-pleasing but in vain.
For, as the wild tornado rips
the branch-bestirring, Taurus-topping   105
oak, or sap-stemmed, cone-filled pine,
and twists with winds the trunk, which falls
uprooted, crushing all below,
so Theseus brought to earth the beast   110
which gored no more than empty air.
Then, following a thread to thwart
the labyrinthine maze, he left
the lair in safety, gloriously.   115
    But why describe, digressing more,
the daughter's flight from a father's face,
a sister's embrace and a mother who
bewailed her ruined daughter's choice
to rejoice in Theseus' charming love,   120
or how she sailed to foaming shores
of Dia, where her husband with
a hardened heart left her in sleep?
They say she raved with flaming heart,

poured forth from her soul words ringing with rage,   125
climbed cliffs in sadness, from whose heights
she viewed the vast expansive sea,
then rushed down into rolling waves,
raising her skirt to bare her legs,
and lifted her last despondent plaints,   130
with chilling sobs and tear-drowned face:
   "So you've left me on this deserted shore
so far from home, ignored the gods
to take home vows whose scorn is cursed,   135
O Theseus, you unfaithful cur.
Could nothing change your vicious mind,
no mercy make your hardened heart
inclined at least to pity me?
These weren't the pretty promises
you made to me; you did not lead
me to expect such grief: the bliss   140
of marriage blown away by winds.
May women never trust man's vows
again, nor hope his words be true:
to reach his soul's goal any man   145
will not forbear to swear or spare
his promises; but, satisfied,
he will not care for breach or fear.
I snatched you from an eddy of death
determined to lose my brother before   150
deserting your deceitful self
in time's decisive moment, which
won me the role of carrion, lost
to burial rites and a cover of earth.
What lion-bitch bore you under a crag,
what sea spat your seed from its spuming waves,   155
what Syrtis, Scylla or crude Charybdis
mothered you, swindler? You owed me your life.

If marrying me disturbed your mind,
fearing your father's rigid rules,
you could have led me to your home   160
to serve you cheerfully and pour
fresh water on your comely feet
and make your bed with purple spread.
Ruined by wrong, oh, why do I wail   165
in vain to the senseless wordless winds?
He is already half over the sea
and no one is here in unpeopled weeds.
So taunting chance denies my cries,   170
in my last hour, an audience.
Almighty Jove, if only first
Cecroprian ships had never touched
our Cnossan shores, the traitor-sailor,
bringing the brutal bull its dole,
had never moored in Crete to rest
as guest with us and hide his hated   175
schemes with handsome mien! Oh, where
to go? what hope to rest on, ruined?
seek out the hills of Crete? the sea
sets us apart; or hope for help
from father, whom I left to chase   180
my brother's bloody murderer?
console myself with my husband's love?
but didn't he row away on the sea?
This island is bare, no roof on the shore,
no path of escape through the circling waves: 185
no exit, no hope: everything's quiet,
everything's empty, everything's dead.
Before my eyes grow dull in death,
my weary body lose its sense,
in my last hour I'll call the gods: 190
Spirits of vengeance on human deeds,

Eumenides, whose serpent hair
exudes your breast-born wrath, come here;
come hear my plaints, which I—dear God!—   195
must utter from my inmost heart,
I, burning, blind with frantic rage.
Since these true plaints come from my heart,
don't let my sorrow fade away;
let Theseus ruin his household in   200
the spirit in which he ruined me!"
    As she hurled these words from her heavy heart
and called a curse on the cruel crimes,
the King of the Gods concurred with a nod
which shook the earth and the shuddering sea   205
while heaven shocked its shining stars.
Theseus, moreover, blinded his mind,
lost sight of the orders remembered before,
nor raised the signs for his father to show   210
that he safely had sighted Athens' port.
They say that when Aegeus, committing his son
to the winds as he left the goddess's walls,
embraced him and gave the following orders:
"My only son, far dearer than life,   215
lately returned to my late old age,
whom I must send off to dubious fates
since my luck, so foul, and your pluck, so fierce,
tear you from my unwilling eyes,
dim and unfilled with the form of my son: 220
I shan't release you and still rejoice
nor let you bear signs of the bloom of success
but shall first express my heartfelt plaints,
pouring dirt and grit on my head's grey hairs,
and hang stained sails to your moving mast   225
that the canvas, dyed with the ochre of Spain,
convey the pains and the heat of my heart.

But if the goddess on holy Itonus [2]
who agreed to defend ourselves and our city
permits you to splatter your hand with the blood   230
of the bull, then take care that these orders remain
in your mind with a strength unstinted by time
that just as soon as you see our hills
your yardarms yield their dismal drape,
your winding ropes hoist whitened sails   235
to let me know great joys as soon
as an untroubled time returns you to me."
These orders, formerly fast in his mind,
left Theseus as gale-driven clouds will leave
the lofty crest of a snowy hill.   240
And Aegeus, straining his anxious eyes
with tireless tears, from his hilltop view
saw the cloth of the swelling sail and jumped
straight from the top of the rocks to the sea,
certain that Theseus was lost to stern fate.   245
So Theseus, arrogant, entered his home,
which his father's funeral darkened, and found
such grief as he'd foisted on Minos' daughter,
who, wounded and gazing woefully toward
the departing ship, pondered manifold cares.   250
From another part of the cloth there flew
flowered Iacchus, with satyrs from Nysa,
in love with and looking, Ariadne, for you.

.   .   .   .

Frantic and fevered, they raved all about
shouting Euhoe and Euhoe, rolling their heads.   255
Some of these shook their sharp stems of vines,
some tossed the limbs of a butchered young bull,
some twined themselves with turntwisting snakes,
some honored secrets in hollow chests:

[2] Reference is again to Athena.

orgies sought vainly by the profane;   260
others with outstretched hands beat drums
or tuned a tattoo with well-turned brass;
bombast was blared by hoarse hollow horns,
and flutes whistled weirdly with sounding song.

    Amply adorned with these figures, the cloth   265
of the vestment enfolded the couch that it veiled.
Once Thessaly's youth had sated its sight
with the figures, the way was cleared for the gods.
Here, as Zephyr's morning breath,
rippling calm waters at Aurora's rise   270
subliminal to the wandering sun,
raises steep waves which roll slowly at first,
with the gentle breeze, sounding laughter-light
but increasing the more with the wind's increase
and reflecting the purple glow from afar: 275
so, leaving the regal porch, the guests
crowd homeward afoot by various paths.

    Chiron came bringing, after they'd gone,
woodland gifts from Pelion's crest:
those flowers which the fields bring forth,
which Thessaly makes on its mighty hills,   280
which the fecund breath of Favonius spawns
by the river waves, were brought by him
woven in wayward garlands, whose
sweet scent amused the house infused.
Peneus takes leave of greengrowing Tempe;   285
Tempe, which binds impendent woods,
he leaves to the Dorian dancing nymphs
and is promptly present, not without gifts:
he has brought uprooted beech trees along,
straight-stemmed bay trees, swaying planes,   290
the pliant poplar and lofty cypress.
These he placed about the palace

to let the leaf-veiled porch grow green.
Brilliant Prometheus follows him
still faintly scarred from the pains of the past   295
which he bore when bound to a rock and chained
in penalty, hung from precipitous cliffs.
Then the Father of Gods arrived
with his blessed wife and progeny,
leaving only Apollo behind in the sky
and his twin,[3] to whom Idrus's hills are home: 300
she spurned Peleus as her brother did,
and refused to honor the wedding of Thetis.

Once they relaxed in the snow-white home
the tables were spread with a manifold feast,
while the Parcae began to prophesy,   305
shaking their bodies with sickly sway.
White garments, wound about their frames,
bound their heels with purple hem;
rose fillets rode their snowy heads;
their hands rightly wrought an unending task: 310
left held the distaff, wound with wool,
right drew threads formed with fingers up,
downturned thumb twisted threads and spun
the spindle balanced by a whirling wheel;
the snapping tooth always smoothed the work,   315
and woolly lint of the light thread clung
to their dried-up lips. At their feet the fleece
of the wool was caught by baskets of twig.
Loudly, plucking the fleece, they sang   320
prophecies free from perfidy:
"Glorious, great-valued spendor and guard
of Emathia, dear to the son of Ops,
hear the sisters' oracular truth   325
revealed on this marvelous day. But now,

[3] Apollo and his twin, i.e., Phoebus and Diana.

spin, you spindles, spin the threads!
    "Hesperus will bring you a bridegroom's hopes,
your bride will come with a lucky star,
she'll fill your mind with a moving love,   330
ready to join you in languid sleep,
her soft arms circling your sturdy neck.
Spin, you spindles, spin the threads!
    "No house ever covered such love,
no love ever bound lovers so well,   335
so perfect to Thetis, to Peleus: the peace.
Spin, you spindles, spin the threads!
    "Fearless Achilles will be your child,
known in a fight by his front, not his back,
very often the victor in races run,   340
beating the burning steps of the stag.
Spin, you spindles, spin the threads!
    "No hero will equal him in war
when Trojan blood floods Phrygian fields   345
and perjured Pelops' third successor
lays low Troy's walls with lengthy war.
Spin, you spindles, spin the threads!
    "Mothers who tear their matted hair   350
and weakly beat their withered breasts
at frequent funerals of their sons
will concede his courage and colorful deeds.
Spin, you spindles, spin the threads!
    "Like the reaper who mows many golden grains
in harvest under the burning sun,
his savage sword will lay Trojans low.   355
Spin, you spindles, spin the threads!
    "Scamander's wave will witness his worth,
filling the Hellespont with heaps of slain
to warm its depths with mingled gore.   360
Spin, you spindles, spin the threads!

"A captive girl [4] will be witness as well
when the rounded mound of a tomb will take
the slaughtered virgin's whitened limbs.
Spin, you spindles, spin the threads!   365
    "For, when Fortune [5] will give the tired Greeks
the means to loosen the Neptune-bonds
of Troy, the tomb for Polyxena
will reek with blood as she bends before
the double axe, like a sacrificed beast
which falls, a bent-kneed, headless corpse.   370
Spin, you spindles, spin the threads!
    "So now unite your loves' desires!
Let husband take goddess in blissful bond,
let bride now take her impatient mate.
Spin, you spindles, spin the threads!   375
    "Yesterday's neckstring, applied by her nurse,
will, in the new dawn, not circle her neck
(Spin, you spindles, spin the threads!)
nor will her mother have to grieve
for a daughter unhappy in her man
and sleeping apart, or despair of heirs.   380
Spin, you spindles, spin the threads!"
    So sang the Parcae to Peleus once:
prophecies of pleasure from heavenly hearts.
For that was when gods, unspurned by neglect,
visited heroes' sinless homes
and showed themselves to assembled men.   385
Looking upon a shining shrine
the Father of Gods would frequently,
during the yearly festivals,
see a hundred bulls sink down to earth.
Liber, away from Parnassus' peak,   390

4 Polyxena.
5 *Fors* (not Fortuna).

often prodded his Thyads, unkempt and in cry,
when Delphians zealously dashed out of town
to welcome, with smoking altars, their god.
Often in deathdealing war would Mars
or the mistress of Triton,[6] or Nemesis,[7]   395
impel, in person, armed companies.
But after the earth was corrupt with crime
and justice gave way to cupidity,
brothers bathed hands in brothers' blood,
a son mourned his buried parents no more,   400
a father desired his first-born's death
to be free to deflower a second wife,
a mother, laid by her unknowing son,
feared not to befoul her parental gods:
the perverted mixture of right and wrong   405
has turned from us the gods' just mind.
And now they avoid men assembled so
and the light of day that mortals know.   408

[6] Again a reference to Athena.
[7] *Ramnusia virgo.*

65

Etsi me assiduo defectum cura dolore

THOUGH worry calls me, wearied by constant grief,
   away from the Learned Girls,[1] Ortalus,
unable mentally to raise the Muses'
   charming brood (such waves of woe:
for, water dripping from Lethe's pool has washed   5
   just now my brother's pallid foot,
whom Troy destroys beneath Rhoeteum's shore,
   whom we can look upon no more.
Brother, more loved than my life, I'll speak   10
   but after this will never hear
you, never see your face; I'll always love
   you, always sing death-saddened songs,
accompanied by the Daulian bird,[2] which mourns
   in dense tree shade the loss of Itys)—
despite such woes, I'm sending you, Ortalus,   15
   translations of Callimachus,[3]
so you won't think your words have fled my mind,
   entrusted to the wandering winds,
as the apple sent by a secret lover rolls
   out of the virgin's spotless lap,   20
cast from its soft concealment by the girl
   thoughtlessly jumping as mother comes;
poor girl; the apple runs its race,
   and blushes bloom upon her face.   24

[1] Namely, the Muses.
[2] The swallow, Procne.
[3] *Battiadae.*

66

Omnia qui magni dispexit lumina mundi

CONON, who conned the lights of the mighty world,
  who learned the risings and settings of stars,
how the flaming gleam of the rapid sun grows dark,
  how the stars depart at certain times,
how sweet love secretly brings Diana down   5
  from gyres of air to Latmos' rocks,
saw likewise me, aglow with heavenly light,
  a lock from the head of Berenice,
which she, with arms outstretched in prayer,
  had promised to many goddesses   10
when her newly-wedded king went out to waste
  the lands of the Assyrians,
showing the signs of the night's sweet fight,
  which he fought for the virgin's spoils.
Is Venus averse to newlyweds? Do tears,   15
  shed falsely in the bridal suite
defeat by fullness, fond parental joys?
  Their groans, so help me gods, are fake!
I learned this from my queen's complaints, with her
  new husband off to screaming wars.   20
Or did you mourn *fraternal* loss with tears
  and not your empty bed at all?
Care ate your bones, to which your grief attained!
  wholly sick at heart and pained,
you lost your sense and mind! I've known   25
  you great-souled as a little girl.
Did you forget the act that none would dare,
  by which you won a royal mate? [1]

[1] See E. M. Merrill (*Catullus* [Boston, 1893], p. 168): "The reference is
doubtless to the story told by Justin (XXVI.3) that Berenice's mother

But what sad words you spoke to see him off!
   God, how sadly you dried your eyes!   30
What great god changed you? Or do lovers hate
   to have their loves a long way off?
And there you promised me, bull's blood as well,
   to all the gods for your dear mate,
if he returned: he shortly took and added   35
   Asia to the lands of Egypt.
Because of this I paid the pristine vow
   and now am in celestial rank.
Unwillingly, O queen, I left your head;
   unwillingly, I swear by you   40
and by your head, which oath let idlers dread:
   but who can prove a match for steel,
which moved the coastland's greatest hill,
   past which the brood of Thia sailed
when Medes broke out a brand new sea and foreign   45
   youth sailed ships through Athos' midst.
When such things yield to steel, what's hair to do?
   God damn the race of Chalybes,
especially him who first sought veins beneath
   the earth and forged the force of steel!   50
My sister locks, bemoaning my fate, saw me
   removed, when Ethiopian Memnon's
brother,[2] the "flying horse" of Locrian [3]
   Arsinoe, came beating the air.
He flies me through the shadows of the sky   55
   to lie on Venus' spotless breast.

---

was opposed to her betrothal to Ptolemy, and desired to marry her
rather to Demetrius, brother of Antigonus, king of Macedonia. De-
metrius, however, formed a criminal connection with the mother, and
was assassinated by a band of conspirators, at whose head stood Berenice,
who thereby was enabled to fulfill her former engagement."

  [2] Memnon = heron; Memnon's brother = ostrich.

  [3] Locrian = "of the West Wind."

Arsinoe, Greek Zephyrite, herself
   had sent her slave from Egypt's shores.
The goddess found me going in tears before
   the temples of the gods and placed   60
me as a star among the stars of old,
   that Ariadne's crown of gold
not shine alone for man, but I as well,
   devoted spoils of yellow hair:
touching the lights of Virgo and savage Leo,   65
   and joined to Callisto, Lycaon's girl,
I lead to west the slow Boötes, who
   sinks late into the Ocean's depth.
Though gods walk over me by night, and day
   restores me to grey Tethys   70
(Ramnusian virgin,[4] let me speak here now;
   I'll never hide the truth through fear,
nor would the slurs of hostile stars keep dark
   the secrets of a proper heart):
these gains find me less pleased than I am pained   75
   at being parted from her head
forever, where I drank the unguents both
   of youth and all the rarer kinds.
Now you, whose marriage hopes are realized,
   who want a righteous marriage bed,
before you bare your breasts and strip and yield   80
   your bodies to your loving men,
let onyx, yes, your onyx send me gifts:
   But she who takes adultery,
bah! let the useless dust drink her damned gifts: 85
   I want no prizes from the shamed.
But brides, ah brides, let concord and constant love
   live always, always in your homes.

4 Nemesis.

You, queen, when eyeing the stars you satisfy
    Venus Divine with festal lamps,   90
don't leave me lacking unguents; I belong
    to you, so send me many gifts.
Let Orion shine next to Aquarius! [5] Let me be
    that regal hair. Stars, let me go!   94

67

O dulci iocunda viro, iocunda parenti

Poet:

Door, dear to a doting husband, dear to his dad,
    hello; God bless you with his help:
they say that you served Balbus very well,
    the time the old boy owned the place;
they also say you served his son like hell,   5
    who, with the old boy dead, was wed:
so tell me, why the change, why is it said
    that you've betrayed the ancient trust?

Door:

To please Caecilius, heir to me, it's not
    my fault, although they say it is,   10
no one can say I've sinned in any way:
    but people say a door does all!
Whenever something wrong has been found out,
    they shout at me, "It's your fault, Door."

Poet:

A word won't do; you'll have to make it clear   15
    enough for anyone to see.

[5] Orion and Aquarius, i.e., Oarion and Hydrochoi.

Door:

How can I? No one asks or tries to learn.

Poet:

I'm asking; tell me—make it quick!

Door:

Well, first: that we received a virgin is a lie.
    Her husband didn't have her first;
his prick, more feeble than a mobile beet,
    has never reached his tunic's midst.
The father screwed the girl in sonny's bed,
    it's said, and stained the poor old house,
his foul mind hot with blinding lust, or else   25
    since seedless sonny couldn't come
and a man was needed, stronger with that tool
    men use to breach a virgin's girdle.

Poet:

Great fatherly love you speak of here, a man
    who'd piss in the married lap of his son!   30

Door:

But this isn't all that Brescia claims to know,
    Brescia beneath Cycnaea's heights,
through which the stream of yellow Mella flows,
    beloved mother of Verona;
she mentions Postumius, Cornelius too,   35
    who found the girl adulterous.
Someone will say, "You know this, Door, when you
    can't leave the owner's threshold or
hear out the people, fastened to a post
    to open or to shut, at most?"   40

I've often heard her whisper to her maids
    about these double-plays of hers;
she named the men I mentioned, free from fear
    that I, the door, could speak or hear.
She named another, whom I'll not disclose   45
    for fear he'd raise his brows (they're red):
he's tall, was once charged with paternity
    in a fictitious pregnancy.   48

68

Quod mihi fortuna casuque oppressus acerbo

BEATEN by luck and bitter chance, you send
   this tearstained letter asking me
to rescue you from shipwreck, as it were,
   and lift you from the door of death,
while holy Venus vetoes gentle rest   5
   and leaves you in a bachelor's bed,
while Muses do not please your anxious mind
   with all the poets' old sweet songs:
I'm pleased, since you will call me friend and ask
   for gifts of Poetry and Love.   10
But, my Allius, I've had my share
   of bad luck: lest you think I'd shirk
the duty of a friend, hear how I've sunk
   in fortune's floods, and ask no favors.
When I first wore unpurpled clothes [1] and bloomed   15
   in childhood's cheerful springtime age,
I played enough and knew the goddess well
   who blends our cares with bittersweetness:
the game was ended by my brother's death;
   I mourn. O brother, you are gone!
Your death has smashed my bank of joy: with you
   our family is now entombed;
with you we've buried all our happiness,
   which your fond living love had fed.
His passing drove these pursuits from my soul   25
   and every pleasure from my mind.
So, what you call a shame, that I am at
   Verona, where a man of note

---

[1] Cf. "short pants" as an emblem of childhood.

must warm cold limbs in a deserted bed,
    call pity, Allius, not shame.   30
And pardon me, if I don't send to you
    grief-ruined gifts, for I cannot.
I have no literary stockpile here,
    because I live at Rome; my home
is there, my house, and there I lead my life;   35
    one pack of books is all that's here.
So, please don't think that it is from ill will
    or lack of generosity
that I've sent neither of the gifts you've asked:
    I'd send both gladly, if I could.   40

Muses, I must say something of the help
    which Allius tendered me, how great
it was, so swift oblivious time will not
    obscure his favor with blind night:
but I'll tell you, and you tell thousands more;   45
    give this poem an old maid's tongue

.   .   .   .

    and let his fame transcend his death,
nor let a lofty spider lift her threads
    across an empty Allius name.   50
Well, you know the pain that two-faced Venus gave
    to me, and how she seared my heart
when I was hot as Etna or the springs
    of Malia in Thermopylae,
my eyes, with constant weeping, dim, my cheeks   55
    wet with a rain of tears: no end.
As a gleaming stream on a mountain crest leaps forth
    from a mossy stone and steeply rolls
from a valley's slope to take its path through crowds
    of people, to relieve the sweat   60

of a weary wanderer, when parched earth cracks
   under heavy heat, and as a wind
with gentle favor breathes on sailors wracked
   and thrown by blackened tempest winds,
praying to Pollux and Castor in distress: 65
   that's how Allius helped me out.
He opened wide a once closed field and gave
   to me and to my love a house
to hold the harvesting of our free love.   70
   There my gleaming goddess, lightly
gliding on the well-worn sill, her sole
   aglow, stopped on squeaking sandals,
as once Laodamia, hot to wed
   entered her Protesilaean home—
no use!—no sacrificial blood had yet   75
   been let, appeasing heaven's lords.
May nothing, Nemesis,[2] please me so much
   that I'd neglect divine assent.
Losing her man, Laodamia learned
   how empty altars yearned for blood,   80
forced to yield her bridegroom's neck before
   one winter coming, and one more,
so filled her fervent love in lengthy nights
   that she could live, with marriage lost:
the Fates knew that the marriage wouldn't last,   85
   once he should fight at Trojan walls:
that's when Troy provoked the first Greek men
   against itself by Helen's rape,
Troy (oh damn) the tomb of East and West
   the bitter bier of men and right: 90
Troy, which brought my brother grievous ruin.
   I mourn: O brother you are gone;

2 *Ramnusia virgo.*

O pleasant light, lost to my poor brother!
   Our family is now entombed
with you, we've buried all our happiness   95
   which your fond living love had fed.
Now far away, by unfamiliar tombs,
   laid near alien ashes in
disgusting Troy, buried in ugly Troy,
   you're fettered in distant, foreign soil.   100
They say that young Greeks hurried there, leaving
   everywhere warm homes behind
so Paris could not gratify his lust
   in a quiet bed of adultery.
Lovely Laodamia, that's why you   105
   lost a husband dearer than
your soul: a love flood whirled a gulf for you
   as deep as soil near Cyllenean
Pheneus, which is rich, Greeks say, because
   its marsh was dried and drained, and which   110
Amphitryon's pseudo-son [3] dug out, they say,
   cutting his way through mountain marrow,
when his arrow drove Stymphalian birds
   away, by order of a lesser lord,
that more gods might rub heaven's door and brief   115
   virginity be Hebe's lot.
But your deep love was deeper than that gulf,
   since it domesticated you.
No only daughter rears a son so dear
   to a grandfather gaining the last of life,   120
a grandson gaining the old man's wealth by signing
   the testate tablets just in time
to scotch the relative's scornful cheer, and drive
   the vulture from the whitened head:

[3] Hercules.

no dove so loved its snowy mate, although   125
   that bird is said to show much more
persistence, plucking constant kisses with
   its beak, than even desire-bent Woman:
no, you transcended passions when you pleased
   your husband of the yellow hair.   130
Less than Laodamia in nothing, the light
   of my soul came into my arms, while here
and there clean Cupid, coursing about her,
   shone clear in his golden garments.
She's not content with just just Catullus, though.   135
   I'll bear her flights from faith—they're few—
and not become too bothersome a pest:
   even Juno, Queen of Heaven,
overlooked her husband's rakishness
   and let her fury simmer down.   140
But it's all wrong, comparing men to gods;

   . . . .

   . . . . it's only fair:
   remove the weight of a fussy father.
She was not led by paternal paw when she,
   sweet with Assyrian scent, found me,
but the gifts she brought that secret night were
      snatched   145
   from the very thighs of her mate himself.
I'm satisfied, if that day which she notes
   on whitened stone is mine alone.

I've done my best with this poetic gift.
   Allius, it's yours for all you've done   150
that this day or that or others and others may not
   crust your name with scabrous rust.
May gods add here as many as they can
   of gifts which Themis used to give

good men. Good luck to you, your wife, the home   155
   which housed my love and me at play.
Good luck to both the lady and man who first
   gave us the world and all good things,
and best of luck to the girl more dear than myself,
   whose life means a lovely life for me.   160

69

Noli admirari, quare tibi femina nulla

DON'T wonder why no woman, Rufe, would want
   to spread her tender thighs for you,
despite your gifts to her of high-class clothes
   and charming bright translucent stones.
There's an ugly rumor that your underarms   5
   are caves for a wild goat's stinking reek.
All are afraid of the goat; no wonder: no *bella*
   puella [1] would share her bed with a beast.
Dispose of this terrible plague to woman's nose,
   or else don't wonder why she runs.   10

70

Nulli se dicit mulier mea nubere malle

MY WOMAN says she'd have me above
   even Jove, if he sought her.
Write woman's words to her man in love
   in wind and swift water.   4

[1] Pretty young girl.

71

Si quoi iure bono sacer alarum obstitit hircus

IF ARMPIT odor ever rightly hurt
 a guy, or gout cut down his speed,
that rival who cuts in on you has gained,
 as he deserved, both maladies.
For, when he screws, he gives you your revenge: 5
 the stink chokes her, the gout kills him.   6

72

Dicebas quondam solum te nosse Catullum

CATULLUS you once called your only love,
 preferred to Jove, my Lesbia.
I loved you, not as men love mistresses,
 but as a father loves his heirs.
I know you now: it makes my love more hot,   5
 but you're more cheap, mere trash to me.
"How so?" you ask. Such dirt heaps up my love
 but buries all my friendliness.   8

73

Desine de quoquam quicquam bene velle mereri

GIVE up the thought of gratitude, the thought
   that men can gain integrity.
Ingratitude prevails, kind acts bring naught;
   in fact they bore, bring enmity:
why, he, who had an "only friend" in me,   5
   now runs me down most bitterly.

74

Gellius audierat patruum obiurgare solere

GELLIUS heard that uncles would complain
   at talk of love or lovers' games.
Preventing this, he pawed his uncle's wife
   and made him an Arpocrates,[1]
and then did as he pleased: for now he gags   5
   his uncle; Unc' won't say a word.   6

75

Huc est mens deducta tua, mea Lesbia, culpa

MY LESBIA, you've brought my heart to this,
   damned by your guilt and its own devotion;
respect is gone, should you become a saint;
   be sin itself, my love can't die.   4

[1] Proverbial for "the quiet type."

76

Si qua recordanti benefacta priora voluptas

IF THERE is any pleasure for a man
   remembering favors past, when he
feels he has kept all faith and formed no bond
   betraying gods to lie to men:
then many joys for many years are yours,   5
   Catullus, for this thankless love.
For, favors men may say or do for men
   have been both said and done by you:
but all was lost in trust to a thankless soul.
   Why suffer more self-torture now?   10
Why not resolve upon retreat from that?—
   the gods say no. Quit courting grief.
It's hard to drop at once a lasting love;
   it's hard, but do it anyway:
this is your only hope, you've got to bring   15
   it off, impossible or not.
Dear gods, if you know pity or bring help
   to souls who feel the pain of death,
look on my pain, and, if my life's been clean,
   take this destructive blight from me!   20
My god, this torpor crawls through all my limbs
   and drains my heart of happiness.
I don't ask for requited love or for
   what cannot be, her decency:
I want to lay aside this foul disease.   25
   Dear gods, restore me through my faith!   26

77

Rufe mihi frustra ac nequiquam credite amice

YOU voided and frustrated, Rufus, my trust
    (frustrated, hell—you busted me good).
Tell me, did you sneak into my life and burn
    my guts to rob my soul's estate?
Hell, sure you did, you poison of my life,   5
    you curse of this our friendship, hell!   6

78

Gallus habet fratres, quorum est lepidissima coniunx

GALLUS has brothers, and one has a wife who is
    delightful, one has a charming son.
Gallus is pretty good, he makes a bed
    of love for the pretty wife and son.
Gallus is foolish, a married uncle himself,   5
    he teaches uncle-cuckolding.   6

78a

Sed nunc id doleo, quod purae pura puellae

. . . .

BUT when my sweetheart's sweetest kisses are mixed
    with the dirty drain of your drool, I'm pained.
You will not get away with it; all time
    will trounce, old fame expose your kind.   4

79

Lesbius est pulcer: quid ni? quem Lesbia malit

Lesbius pretty? [1] Sure. And Lesbia loves
   him more than you and all your kin,
Catullus; but let him sell Catullus and kin,
   if he can win three worthy loves.   4

80

Quid dicam, Gelli, quare rosea ista labella

Gellius, I'll tell you why your rosy lips
   get whiter than winter snow: you go
out early, living it up in luscious rest
   until the summer afternoon.
Does rumor whisper right to say you bite   5
   erected loins? This isn't clear.
But little Victor's violated rear
   and your marked lips are amply clear.   8

[1] *Lesbius est pulcer: Pulc(h)er* means "pretty" or "good-looking"; it is also the cognomen of Publius Clodius Pulcher, the supposed Lesbius of this poem, just as his sister Clodia is the supposed Lesbia of this and other poems.

81
▟▚▚▞▚▞▞▞▞

Nemone in tanto potuit populo esse, Iuventi

I<small>N</small> <small>ALL</small> the world, Juventius, couldn't you
   have found some dude on whom to dote
besides that dead Pisaurian polly, who
   is paler than a statue's coat?
He's won your heart, whom now you dare to place   5
   above me, blind to your disgrace.   6

82
▚▞▚▞▚▞▚▞▚▞▚▞

Quinti, si tibi vis oculos debere Catullum

Q<small>UINTIUS,</small>
   do you want Catullus to owe you his eyes
   or what he would prize above them?
Don't take what he treasures more than his eyes
   or what he would treasure above them.   4

83

Lesbia mi praesente viro mala plurima dicit

LESBIA, with her man [1] around, always runs me in the
  ground:
        the fool takes this as perfect bliss.
You ass, you're crass; she'd be all right, forgetting me,
  to clam up tight;
        but while she speaks with vicious hiss,
not only am I kept in mind, I plant the anger she will   5
  find
        as love's loquacious nemesis.   6

84

"Chommoda" dicebat, si quando "commoda" vellet

C-HOMMODE" for "commode" Arrius would say
  and "hambush" for "ambush,"
and think it most stylish in every way
  to aspirate: "hambush."
So spoke his mother, his uncle, and so   5
  his maternal grandparents.
He went to the East and our ears then heard
  the sounds of these words,
now smooth and precise. We feared them no more.
  But then came the news   10
that Ionian seas were no longer "Ionian,"
  but, in Arrian, "Hionian."   12

[1] Lesbia's husband, assuming that she was the famous Clodia, would
be Q. Metellus Celer, a Roman consul who died in 59 B.C.

85

Odi et amo. quare id faciam, fortasse requiris

I HATE while I love; would you ask how I do it? My pain
proves it's true; that's all there is to it.   2

86

Quintia formosa est multis, mihi candida, longa

QUINTIA's a "dream" to many, to me: bright, tall,
quite straight; I'll grant each single trait.
But the big girl isn't a "dream"; that's all:
no charm or spark for her weight.
Lesbia's a "dream" in every respect; she'll glean   5
all rivals' charms and strip them clean.   6

87

Nulla potest mulier tantum se dicere amatam

No WOMAN can claim to have known the love
that Lesbia knew from me.
No bond of faith was ever so strong
as mine, with your love the key.   4

88

Quid facit is, Gelli, qui cum matre atque sorore

GELLIUS, what's with a guy who tickles his mother
and sister all night, without tunic or panty?
What's with a guy who keeps his uncle from auntie?
    Have you any idea how evil he is?
O Gelly, not faraway Tethys or Ocean,   5
    the father of nymphs, can cleanse his sins:
no evil could surpass his incestuous pelf,
    not even if he could suck himself.   8

89

Gellius est tenuis: quid ni? cui tam bona mater

GELLIUS is skinny: why not? he has so fine,
    so strong a mom, so sweet a sis,
so fine an uncle and so full a herd
    of female cousins. Sure, he's thin!
His hands are never where they ought to be.   5
    That's why he's so thin. You'll see.   6

90

Nascatur magus ex Gelli matrisque nefando

LET a potential Persian prophet come
    from Gellius' marriage with his mom:
a prophet's parents, you see, are mother and son,
    if Persians' perverted beliefs are true,
so he can please the gods with hymns of praise   5
    melting the wrapper of fat in flame.   6

91

Non ideo, Gelli, sperabam te mihi fidum

GELLIUS, I didn't hope for faith from you
   in this my lost, my lonely love,
because I thought you right or regular
   or able to relax your lust,
but since the girl, the love of whom consumed me,   5
   was not your mother or your sister.
Although I knew you from experience,
   I didn't think you'd find your thrill.
You did, delighting as you do in guilt
   of any kind, in any wrong.   10

92

Lesbia mi dicit semper male nec tacet umquam

LESBIA loves to libel me, endlessly;
   but she loves me I'm damned sure,
for I pay her back with dirty cracks, constantly,
   and damned if I don't love her.   4

93

Nil nimium studeo, Caesar, tibi velle placere

MY DESIRE to please you, Caesar, is slight, nor do
   I care to know if you're black or white.   2

94

> *"Mentula moechatur." moechatur mentula certe*

MANTOOL [1] fornicates; he fornicates: why not?
You know what they say: "For potherbs, a pot!"   2

95

> *Zmyrna mei Cinnae nonam post denique messem*

NINE winters after the work was first begun
my Cinna has published his *Zmyrna* at last;
Hortensius, meanwhile, writes thousands of lines in one

. . . .

The *Zmyrna* will reach the Satrach's channeled waves,   5
be read when centuries have passed.
But Volusius' annals will die in Padua
as ample and frequent wrappers for fish.
My Cinna's works are few but dear; let people
cheer the stuffed Antimachus.   10

---

[1] The word *mentula* means "penis." It is used as a proper name here
and in poems 105, 114, and 115. It is used as a common noun in poems 29, 37.

96

Si quicquam mutis gratum acceptumve sepulcris

CALVUS, if our grief can give the grave
    any satisfactory cheer
in heartache, which renews old loves to save
    lost friendships with our every tear,
Quintilia's early death will bring less grief   5
    to her than your love brings relief.   6

97

Non (ita me di ament) quicquam referre putavi

GODS love me, I can't rightly tell which hole
    I'd smell in Emil,[1] mouth or ass.
It's hard to say, but I would judge the ass
    wins out for cleanliness and class:
it has no teeth. The mouth has half a yard   5
    of gums that grate like wagon crates;
it widens as, in summer, split in two,
    the cunt of a pissing mule will do.
He screws the girls and preens himself with charm—
    and isn't on a donkey farm?   10
The girl who touches him would kiss the stink
    of some sick hangman's ass, I think.   12

[1] *Aemilius.*

98

In te, si in quemquam, dici pote, putide Victi

STINKING Victius,
    to you, if anyone, that can be said
which people say to loudmouthed louts:
    that tongue of yours could wipe an ass or clean
    a farmer's shoe, had you the chance.
Suppose you want to see us dead and gone: 5
    to get your wish, just yawn, man, yawn.   6

99

Surrupui tibi, dum ludis, mellite Iuventi

JUVENTIUS, you played and I stole a kiss
    sweeter than sweet ambrosia.
It wasn't free: you crucified me,
    I remember, more than an hour.
I failed with excuses and tears to curb   5
    your cruelty even slightly.
You promptly doused your lips and rubbed
    them roughly with every finger,
as though I had left such germs as does
    the putrid drool of a whore.   10
What's more, you wouldn't forbear to leave
    me tortured and ravaged by love
till the sweet kiss changed to one that was
    harsher than harsh hellebore.
Since you punish my poor love so, I shall   15
    steal kisses from you no more.   16

100

Caelius Aufilenum et Quintius Aufilenam

AUFILENUS is Aufilena's brother;
   they're the bloom of Veronese youth.
Quintius loves the girl, Caelius the other:
   a "sweet fraternal pact," in truth.
My favorite? Caelius, you: your acts were loans   5
   of heart that only friendship knew
when poisoned fire parched my very bones.
   Good luck and all love's strength to you.   8

101

Multas per gentes et multa per aequora vectus

I'VE sailed to many nations over many seas
   and come now, brother, to this final rite,
these obsequies, to honor you in death and say
   a word or two at unresponsive ash,
since fate, where I'm concerned, has been so rash   5
   as uselessly to hasten you away.
So take this customary family mite—
   our mourning duty, offerings like these:
they're moistened with your brother's many tears.
   Goodbye for now: farewell for all the years.   10

102

Si quicquam tacito commissum est fido ab amico

CORNELIUS, you'll find me bound by oaths
 that friends conjure in silent trust
with those whose faith of soul is deeply stamped.
 Consider me Arpocrates.[1]   4

103

Aut sodes mihi redde decem sestertia, Silo

SILO, supply, please, my ten sesterces,
 and then be as vicious and wild as you will:
should the coins charm too much, cease pimping it, please,
 remaining as vicious and wild as you will.   4

104

Credis me potuisse meae maledicere vitae

YOU think I could curse the girl whom I prize
 more than my life or my eyes?
I couldn't if I could, I love her so much:
 you and Tappo tell all your damn lies.   4

---

[1] See poem 74.

105

Mentula conatur Pipleium scandere montem

MANTOOL[1] tries to scale Pipleius' crest: the
Muses' pitchforks send him to his rest.   2

106

Cum puero bello praeconem qui videt esse

SEEING a salesman with a fine young male, one
thinks the boy means, "I'm for sale."   2

107

Si quoi quid cupido optantique optigit umquam

IF EVER, lacking expectation, one
has hopes fulfilled, his soul is pleased.
And so I'm pleased that you, my Lesbia,
my precious hope, return to me
as I desired but could not quite expect: 5
O golden day of gleaming note!
Who lives more blest than I, or finds in life
a finer base for hopes than this?   8

[1] See poem 94.

108

Si, Comini, populi arbitrio tua cana senectus

COMINIUS,
   if your grey age, defiled by filthy fads,
  should end by popular demand,
I have no doubt your antisocial tongue,
  cut out, would scrve a vulture's greed,
a crow's black throat would gulp your picked-out eyes,   5
  a dog your guts, and wolves the rest.   6

109

Iocundum, mea vita, mihi proponis amorem

MY LIFE, you say this love of ours will be
   requited through eternity.
Great gods, please grant that she can give her word
  in truth and all sincerity,
that we might know throughout the life we lead   5
  our sacred friendship's surety.   6

110

Aufilena, bonae semper laudantur amicae

AUFILENA,
    faithful frails are always praised: they're paid
and carry out what they propose.
You lie and break the promises you've made;
    all take, no give: that's criminal.
An ingenue would give, a modest girl   5
    not promise: grabbing gifts by fraud
is worse a crime than that of any bawd
    who sells her body and her soul.   8

111

Aufilena, viro contentam vivere solo

AUFILENA,
    married women's praise of praises lies
in love of husband and no other,
but lie with anyone you wish before
    your own first cousin calls you mother.   4

112

Multus homo es, Naso, neque tecum multus homo est, qui

YOU'RE a made man, Naso, nor is he who lays you made:
    you're a made man, Naso, and a—maid.   2

113

Consule Pompeio primum duo, Cinna, solebant

IN POMPEY'S first consulship, Cinna, two men
  knew Maecilia; now that he's consul again,
the two have remained but have each bred a breed
  of thousands, with fertile adulterous seed.   4

114

Firmanus saltus non falso, Mentula, dives

MANTOOL,[1]
  they're right who say your Firman glen is rich,
  with its outstanding qualities,
its game birds, varied fish, fields, meadows, beasts.
  No use: its debt exceeds its gain.
I'll grant it's rich, while he is destitute;   5
  let's praise his glen, but not his pain.   6

[1] See poem 94.

115

Mentula habet instar triginta iugera prati

MANTOOL [1] has some thirty meadow acres,
forty of farmland, a sea of others.
Why can't he be richer than Croesus, with so many pieces
of assets and profits in one estate,
meadows, farmlands, forests, glens and swamps   5
north and west to the end of the world?
Great as these are, there is one thing greater yet,
not man, but a mantool (what a threat!).   8

116

Saepe tibi studioso animo venante requirens

SEARCHING to serve your interests with a gift
of poems of Callimachus,[1]
to soften you toward me, so you'd not try
to brain me with your hostile spears,
I see I undertook the task in vain   5
and wasted, Gellius, all my prayers.
I'll use my cloak to turn aside your spears,
but, pierced by mine, you'll pay with pain.   8

1 See poem 94.
1 *Battiadae.*

FRAGMENTS

See Poem 18.

Preserved by Nonius Marcellus:
> *. . . de meo ligurrire libido est.*
> . . . for my part, sucking is sweet.

Preserved by Porphyrius in his comment on Horace's ode (1.16,22):
> *At non effugies meos iambos.*
> But you will not escape my verse.

INDEX OF PERSONAL NAMES[1]

---

[1] Reference is made to the poems and line numbers of the Latin and to the page numbers of this translation; for example, "*74:* 4; *102:* 4; pp. 94, 107" indicates that the name is found in poem 74 (line 4) and poem 102 (line 4) of the original Latin, the line numbers of which are used in this translation; "pp. 94, 107" refers to the pages of this book.

parently enjoined his wor-
shipers to silence. *74:* 4; *102:*
4; pp. 94, 107.

ARRIUS. Lawyer; contemporary
of Catullus. *84:* 2, 11; p. 99.

ARSINOE. Sister and wife of
Ptolemy II, Philadelphus
(reigned 285-247 B.C.), equated
with Venus-Arsinoe by her
descendants. *66:* 54; p. 81.

ASINIUS MARRUCINUS. Brother of
C. Asinius Pollio. *12:* 1; p. 13.

ATALANTA. The swiftest runner
on earth. She promised to
marry the man who defeated
her in a foot race. Unsuccess-
ful suitors were to forfeit their
lives. Hippomenes (or Melan-
ion) defeated her by throw-
ing golden apples in her path.
He passed her each time she
broke stride to retrieve one.
P. 2.

ATHENA. See Minerva.

ATTIS. Mythical Greek youth who
emasculated himself in wor-
ship of Cybele. *63:* 1, 27, 32,
42, 45, 88; pp. 63-65.

AUFILENA. Veronese girl, con-
temporary of Catullus. *100:* 1;
110: 1; *111:* 1; pp. 106, 110.

AUFILENUS. Veronese man; con-
temporary of Catullus; brother
of Aufilena. *100:* 1; p. 106.

AURELIUS. Male contemporary of
Catullus. *11:* 1; *15:* 2; *16:* 2;
21: 1; pp. xiv, 12, 16, 17, 22.

AURORA. Dawn (goddess). *64:*
271; p. 74.

AURUNCULEIA. Vinia or Junia
Aurunculeia; bride of Manlius

Torquatus. *61:* 16, 86; pp. 52,
55.

BACCHANTE. A female worshiper
of Bacchus. *64:* 60; p. 68.

BACCHUS. Dionysus, Liber, Thyo-
neus; god of wine and fertility.
27: 7; *64:* 251, 390; pp. x, 26,
73.

BALBUS. Widower; belonging to
the generation before Catul-
lus. *67:* 3; p. 83.

BATTIADES, -AE. Son or descend-
ant of a Battus. See Calli-
machus.

BATTUS. Legendary founder of
Cyrene in Libya. *7:* 6; p. 8.

BERENICE. Daughter of King
Magas of Cyrene; wife of
Ptolemy III, Euergetes (king
of Egypt, 247-222 B.C.). *66:* 8;
pp. 80 f.

BOOTES. The constellation; also
called Arcturus. *66:* 67; p. 82.

BOREAS. God or king of the
north wind. *26:* 3; p. 26.

CAECILIUS. Latin poet; younger
friend of Catullus. *35:* 2, 18;
p. 33.

CAECILIUS. Veronese man; con-
temporary of Catullus. *67:* 9;
p. 83.

CAELIUS. A friend of Catullus;
possibly M. Caelius Rufus, de-
fended by Cicero in 56 B.C. If
so, it is Catullus' friend, then,
who alienates the affection of
Lesbia (cf. Caelius Rufus' con-
nection with Clodia in Cicero's
Pro Caelio; see poems 59, 69,
73, 77). *58:* 1; pp. viii, ix, xi, 50.

CAELIUS. Veronese man; friend of Catullus; possibly the Caelius mentioned above. *100:* 1, 5, 8; p. 106.

CAESAR, C. JULIUS. 102-44 B.C.; conqueror of Gaul, dictator, historian. *11:* 10; *57:* 2; *93:* 1 (cf. *29* and *54*); pp. viii, ix, xi, xii, 12, 28, 47, 49, 102.

CAESIUS. Poet; contemporary of Catullus. *14:* 18; p. 15.

CALLIMACHUS. Alexandrian poet; contemporary of Ptolemy II, III (Philadelphus and Euergetes); chief librarian of library at Alexandria from about 260 to 240 B.C.; see Berenice. Poem 66 is a Catullan translation of one of his works. *65:* 16; *116:* 2; pp. 79, 112.

CALLISTO. Daughter of Lycaon; changed into a bear, then a constellation. *66:* 66; p. 82.

CALVUS, C. LICINIUS. 82-46 B.C.; lawyer and poet; very close friend of Catullus. *14:* 2; *50:* 1, 8; *53:* 3; *96:* 2; pp. viii-x, xiv, 15, 45, 47, 104.

CAMERIUS. Friend of Catullus at Rome. *55:* 10; *58a:* 7; pp. 48, 50.

CAMISOLE. See Camerius.

CASTOR. Twin brother of Pollux; son of Leda and Tyndareus. *4:* 27; *68:* 65; pp. 5, 35, 88.

CATO. Friend of Catullus; possibly Valerius Cato, Veronese poet and grammarian. *56:* 1, 3; p. 49.

CATULLUS, C. VALERIUS. 87/84-about 54 B.C.; Veronese poet.

6: 1; *7:* 10; *8:* 1, 12, 19; *10:* 25; *11:* 1; *13:* 7; *14:* 13; *38:* 1; *44:* 3; *46:* 4; *49:* 4; *51:* 13; *52:* 1, 4; *56:* 3; *58:* 2; *68:* 27, 135; *72:* 1; *76:* 5; *79:* 2, 3; *82:* 1; pp. vii-xvi, 7-9, 11, 12, 14-15, 19, 33-34, 36, 41, 43-44, 46, 48-50, 90, 93, 95, 97-98.

CECROPS. An ancestor of the Athenians; great grandfather of Theseus. Cecropian = Athenian. *61:* 79, 83, 172; pp. 68, 71.

CELER, Q. METELLUS. See p. 99.

CHALYBES. A nation living on the south coast of the Black Sea. *66:* 48; p. 81.

CHARYBDIS. Daughter of Poseidon (Neptune); ship-swallowing whirlpool in the straits of Messina. *64:* 156; p. 70.

CHIRON. A centaur. *64:* 279; p. 74.

CICERO, MARCUS TULLIUS. 106-43 B.C.; rhetorician, lawyer, politician; Rome's greatest orator. *49:* 2; pp. viii, xi, 44.

CINNA, C. HELVIUS. Poet; close friend of Catullus. *10:* 30; *95:* 1; *113:* 1; pp. 11, 103, 111.

CLODIA (or Claudia). Sister of P. Clodius Pulcher (Lesbius?); wife of Q. Metellus Celer; reputed to have been debauched, a nymphomaniac, poisoner of her husband; very possibly the Lesbia whom Catullus loved and lost. See pp. ix, xi, 97, 99.

CLODIUS (or Claudius). P. Clodius Pulcher, brother of Clodia; Tribune of the People in 58 B.C.; henchman of Caesar;

enemy of Cicero; profligate, but popular. See pp. ix, 97.

COMINIUS. Unknown male contemporary of Catullus; apparently an old lecher. *108:* 1; p. 109.

CONON. Alexandrian mathematician; friend of Archimedes; born at Samos; flourished about 250 B.C. *66:* 2; p. 80.

CORNELIUS. Unknown male contemporary of Catullus; possibly Cornelius Nepos. *102:* 4; p. 107.

CORNELIUS. Unknown male contemporary of Catullus; native of Brescia (Latin *Brixia*). *67:* 35; p. 84.

CORNELIUS NEPOS. About 99-24 B.C.; Roman historian; Veronese; good friend of Catullus. *1:* 3; p. 3.

CORNIFICIUS. Poet; younger friend of Catullus. *38:* 1; p. 36.

CROESUS. King of Lydia (560-546 B.C.); his wealth was proverbial. *115:* 3; p. 112.

CUPID (or Amor [Love]). The son of Venus. *3:* 1; *13:* 12; *36:* 3; *45:* 8, 17; *68:* 133; *99:* 11; pp. 4, 14, 34, 42, 90, 105.

CYBELE. A Phrygian goddess; also called *Magna Mater* (Great Mother). *63:* 9, 12, 20, 35, 68, 76, 84, 91; pp. 33, 63-65.

DAWN STAR. See Eous.

DEMETRIUS. Brother of Antigonus Gonatas; lived in Cyrene. See p. 80.

DIANA. Goddess of chastity and hunting; equated with the moon (Luna); sister of Apollo (Phoebus, the sun); also called Juno Lucina, Latonia, Trivia. *34:* 1, 3; cf. *64:* 300; pp. 32, 75, 80.

DIONE. Mother of Venus; also equated with Venus. *56:* 6; p. 49.

EGNATIUS. Male contemporary of Catullus; a Spaniard. *37:* 19; *39:* 1, 9; pp. xiv, 35, 37.

EMIL. See Aemilius.

EOUS. Lucifer, the morning star. *62:* 35; p. 61.

EUMENIDES. The Furies, forces of conscience. *64:* 193; p. 72.

FABULLUS. Close friend of Catullus. *12:* 15, 17; *13:* 1, 14; *28:* 3; *47:* 3; pp. 13 f., 27, 43.

FATES. See Parcae.

FAVONIUS. The west wind, Zephyr. *26:* 2; *64:* 282; pp. 26, 74.

FIDES. Goddess of faith and trust. *30:* 11; p. 29.

FLAVIUS. Unknown male friend of Catullus. *6:* 1; p. 7.

FORMIAN. A resident of Formia; possibly Mamurra (cf. Mentula). *41:* 4; *43:* 5; pp. 38, 40.

FORS. Goddess of chance or fortune. *64:* 170, 366; pp. 71, 77.

FURIUS. Unknown male contemporary of Catullus. *11:* 1; *16:* 2; *23:* 1, 24; *26:* 1; pp. xiv, 12, 17, 24, 26.

GALLAE. Castrated worshipers of Cybele; followers of Attis. *63:* 12, 34; pp. 63-64.

GALLUS. Unknown male contemporary of Catullus. *78:* 1, 3, 5; p. 96.

GELLIUS. One of Catullus' rivals for the affection of Lesbia. *74:* 1; *80:* 1; *88:* 1, 5; *89:* 1; *90:* 1; *91:* 1; *116:* 6; pp. xiv, xv, 94, 97, 101 f., 112.

HAMADRYADS. Tree nymphs. *61:* 23; p. 52.

HARRY. See Herius and note p. 47.

HEBE. Goddess of youth; divine wife of Hercules. *68:* 116; p. 89.

HELEN. Wife of Menelaus; raped (kidnaped) by Paris. *68:* 87; p. 80.

HELIOS. The sun god; warden of the south wind. *26:* 3; p. 26.

HERCULES. Son of Alcmene and Jupiter, stepson of Amphitryon; one of his famous Twelve Labors was the capture of Hippolyta's girdle. *55:* 13; pp. 48, 89.

HERIUS (Marrucinus). Unknown male contemporary of Catullus. *54:* 2; p. 47.

HESPERUS. Vesper, the evening star. *62:* 20, 26, 32, 35; *64:* 329; pp. 60 f., 76.

HORACE. Q. Horatius Flaccus, 65-8 B.C.; one of the greatest names in Roman poetry. Pp. vii, 113.

HORTENSIUS. See Ortalus.

HYDROCHOI. The constellation Aquarius. *66:* 94; p. 94.

HYMEN. God of marriage. *61* (throughout); *62:* (through-

out); *66:* 67; pp. 52-62. HYMENAEUS = marriage song or marriage.

IACCHUS. See Bacchus.

IO. Daughter of the river god Inachus; she was seduced by Jupiter and subsequently transformed into a white heifer. P. x.

IPSITILLA. A prostitute known to Catullus. *32:* 1; p. 31.

ITYS. Son of Tereus and Procne; butchered, stewed, and fed to Tereus by Procne in revenge for Tereus' rape and mutilation of her sister Philomela. *65:* 14; p. 79.

JOVE. See Jupiter.

JUNO. Sister and wife of Jupiter; queen of the gods. *68:* 138; p. 90. Lucina Juno or Juno Lucina is Diana.

JUPITER. King of the gods, father of gods and men; also known as Jove. *1:* 7; *4:* 20; *7:* 5; *34:* 6; *55:* 5; *64:* 26, 171; *66:* 30, 48; *67:* 2; *68:* 140; *70:* 2; *72:* 2; pp. 3, 5, 8, 32, 48, 67, 71, 81, 83, 90, 92 f.

JUVENTIUS. A young man, perhaps a ward of Catullus; he was the object of homosexual attention on the part of Catullus. *24:* 1; *48:* 1; *81:* 1; *99:* 1; pp. viii, xi, xii, xiv, 25, 44, 98, 108.

LADAS. A famous Spartan footracer. *58a:* 3; p. 50.

LAODAMIA. Wife of Protesilaus. *68:* 74, 80, 105; p. 88 f.

LATONIA = Diana. Daughter of Latona. *34:* 5; p. 32.

PHOEBUS. Apollo, sun god and brother of Diana. *64:* 299; p. 75.

PISO. A Roman propraetor (provincial governor); probably L. Calpurnius Piso Caesoninus (Roman consul in 58 B.C.; governor of Macedonia in 57-55 B.C.). *28:* 1; *47:* 2; pp. 27, 43.

POLLIO, C. ASINIUS. 76-5 B.C.; lawyer; poet; brother of Asinius Marrucinus. *12:* 6; p. 13.

POLLUX. Twin brother of Castor; son of Leda and Jupiter. *68:* 65; pp. 5, 35, 88.

POLYXENA. Daughter of King Priam of Troy; slain in sacrifice on the tomb of Achilles. *64:* 368; p. 77.

POMPEY (Cnaeus Pompeius Magnus [the Great]). 106-48 B.C.; Roman general; consul in 70 and again in 55 B.C.; made public his theater and adjoining portico during his second consulship. *55:* 6; *113:* 1; pp. viii, 48, 111.

PORCIUS. Unknown male contemporary of Catullus. *47:* 1; p. 43.

PORKY. See Porcius.

PORPHYRIUS (or Porphyry). Greek philosopher (Neoplatonist) and scholar; born 233 A.D. P. 113.

POSTUMIA. Unknown woman, named by Catullus as the master of a feast. Such a feast, with a *woman* as master, would be an orgy of the wildest type. *27:* 3; p. 26.

POSTUMIUS. Unknown native of Brescia (Latin *Brixia*) during Catullus' time. *67:* 35; p. 84.

PRIAPUS. See p. 19. *18:* 1, 2; *20:* 17, 20; *47:* 4; pp. 19-21.

PROCNE. Daughter of Pandion; sister of Philomela; wife of Tereus, who raped Philomela and cut out her tongue; mother of Itys. See p. 79.

PROMETHEUS. Son of the Titan Iapetus; champion of mankind; chained to Mount Caucasus and tortured for defying Jupiter. *64:* 294; p. 75.

PROTESILAUS. The first Greek to be killed in the Trojan War; husband of Laodamia. *68:* 74; p. 88.

PTOLEMY. See Berenice.

QUINTIA. Unknown female contemporary of Catullus. *86:* 1; p. 100.

QUINTILIA. Female relative (or possibly the sweetheart) of C. Licinius Calvus. *96:* 6; p. 104.

QUINTIUS. Unknown male contemporary of Catullus; Veronese. *82:* 1; *100:* 1; pp. xiv, 98, 106.

RAMNUSIA. See Nemesis.

RAVIDUS. One of Catullus' rivals for the affection of Lesbia. *40:* 1; pp. xiv, 38.

REMUS. Brother of Romulus, legendary founder of Rome. *28:* 15; *58:* 5; pp. 27, 50.

RHESUS. King of Thrace during the Trojan War. *58a:* 4; p. 50.

INDEX OF GEOGRAPHICAL NAMES[1]

[1] No distinction is made between nominal and adjectival forms of the names listed. Readers who are interested in Catullus' geographical allusions will want to consult the Everyman's Library *Atlas of Ancient and Classical Geography* (useful maps) along with *A Dictionary of Greek and Roman Geography* (2 volumes, edited by Wm. Smith, London, 1873, 1878; thoroughgoing details).

INDEX OF FIRST LINES (LATIN)